The Bargain Hunter's
[& Smart Consumer's]
Field Guide

How To Buy Almost Anything For Next To Nothing

Art Beroff and Rob & Terry Adams

Avebury Books
P.O. Box 27309
Panama City Beach, FL 32411

Quantity discounts are available for bulk purchases of this book for educational or gift purposes, or as premiums for businesses and professional organizations. Special books or book excerpts can be created to fit specific needs. For information, please contact Avebury Books, P.O. Box 27309, Panama City Beach, FL 32411, (850) 636-4006.

Cataloging-in-Publication Data

Beroff, Art
The bargain hunter's & smart consumer's field guide: how to buy just about anything for next to nothing / by Art Beroff and Rob & Terry Adams.

    p. cm.
    Includes index.
    ISBN: 0-9714598-1-9
    1. Shopping—United States. 2. Consumer education—United States. 3. Entrepreneurship. 4. Finance—personal. 5. Real estate—purchasing. I. Adams, Rob. II. Adams, Terry. III. Title.

First Edition

This book is dedicated to my wife Carole. As an attorney for the Department of Consumer Affairs, she has spent most of her professional career helping the people of New York keep our great city consumer-friendly and safe from unscrupulous merchants.

Art Beroff

This one's for Gregg and Roger. Thanks for being there!

Rob & Terry Adams

Table Of Contents

Introduction

Everybody loves a BARGAIN. Everyone likes being a smart consumer. There's the financial satisfaction of saving money, and there's also the creative satisfaction of seeking out and shaping a deal that no one else has discovered.

That's what this book is about. It's not about where to find bargains—they're anywhere and everywhere. Instead, it's about how to obtain them. Within these pages, we reveal the SECRETS of SUCCESSFUL bargain hunting. Not only at discount outlets and warehouse centers, but at regular merchants where only the savvy dare to deal. At antique malls and auctions. And in private-party transactions from garage sales to garaged vehicles.

This book gives you the tools to search out real bargains in both likely and unlikely places and to deal your way to fantastic and seemingly unbelievable buys. If you're already a bargain-hunter, you'll find yourself in BUYER'S BLISS; if you're one of the haggle-phobic, take heart. You'll learn how to Walk the Walk and Talk the Talk. And you'll learn how to make it a win-win situation, so that both you and the seller come away happy. No hard feelings, no guilt. Just what you bargained for.

[Every dollar you save—or ten dollars or one hundred or one thousand dollars—by shopping smart is a dollar in your bank account that you wouldn't otherwise have, a dollar you'd have to spend extra time and effort to earn (and then pay income tax on).]

Real bargain hunting is a terrific way to stretch your purchasing dollar and save time as well as money. Every dollar you save—or ten dollars or one hundred or one thousand dollars—by shopping smart is a dollar in your bank account that you wouldn't otherwise have, a dollar you'd have to spend extra time and effort to earn (and then pay income tax on). It doesn't matter if you're a prince or a pauper-on-the-way-up, this is true for everyone.

As a bargain hunter, you can not only stretch your buying dollars but also make them more powerful than you might think possible. Suddenly you'll find you can afford those extra amenities. You can remodel your house, refurnish your apartment, put a set of snazzy wheels in your driveway, equip your home and business with computers and electronics, and give splashy gifts—all while keeping well within your monetary means.

Bargain hunting is also a heck of a lot of fun, as irresistible as caffeine or chocolate—and it puts a lot less stress on your nerves and waistline. It's also smart consumerism that saves you from making wrong decisions on wrong products and services.

As a savvy bargain hunter and consumer, you'll learn to buy the things you want and need for a fraction of the regular price. But you'll also learn when to pass up things that aren't good deals, and even those that are when you can't really afford them. Guilt-free shopping!

About This Book

Whether you're buying for yourself, your family, or your company, you'll learn lots, including how to:

* Get discounts and unadvertised specials everywhere you shop
* Get merchants to call you when deals come in
* Use the Internet to get bargain prices at local merchants as well as online

 The Bargain Hunter's [& Smart Consumer's] Field Guide

✳ Get discounts from service providers—doctors, attorneys insurance companies, contractors, and more
✳ Negotiate great deals on family and business vehicles
✳ Find the real deals at flea markets, garage sales, and auctions
✳ Negotiate like a millionaire on real estate property
✳ Make your business look like a million bucks on a shoestring

How To Use This Book

We've designed this book to be easy, fun, and practical. Read it cover to cover from page one, start at the end and work your way forward, or dip into it at any page that strikes your interest. (Unlike murder mysteries and thrillers, reading the end first won't spoil the plot.)

Use this book just as the title implies, as a field guide for your own personal and business buying success. You'll find special chapters on buying cars, real estate, and services, on shopping online, in bulk and wholesale, and on hunting antiques, consignment goods, and other pre-owned treasures. You'll also find special "Business Beacons" for entrepreneurs and small-business people. Flip directly to the section that fits your needs, then get shopping—and saving!

We've included the **Twelve Secrets of the Bargain Seeker**— the ultimate bargain hunter's tools—for your use, as well as a wealth of tip boxes, sidebars, and fun facts to help you become an expert bargain hunter and smart consumer in no time.

About Us

We've developed these tools and techniques over the course of a combined 50 years of successful bargain-hunting. We've bought everything from home improvement products to computers to comforters at up to ninety percent off retail. We've made money on every car we've purchased—after driving it for a year or more first. We've equipped our offices and purchased business products and services at tremendous savings. And we've negotiated terrific bargains in real estate.

About You

You can do the same thing. If you've picked up this book, you've taken the first step toward becoming a successful bargain hunter and savvy consumer. You're putting your feelers out. You're doing research. And you're evincing two of the bargain-hunter's most important traits: curiosity and creativity. You've got the right stuff.

So what are you waiting for? Turn the page!

Chapter One
Seekers Of The Hidden Bargain

Most people have no idea that great deals surround them every time they shop. Whether they're looking for computers, clothing, infant car seats, or carpet, if they want a bargain they have to wait until a store announces a sale.

Mention "bargain" to the average shopper and you conjure up visions of discount centers and dim department store basements—or hours spent clipping coupons. But the true bargain hunter—a swash-buckling archaeologist/adventurer of another kind—knows the many mysteries hidden within the stockrooms of regular retailers and, what's more, knows how to unearth them.

Real bargain hunting is an art, a quest, and a game. It's spotting a sale before it's official. Sniffing out a deal that doesn't yet exist. And creating bargains where most people see only marked-up merchan-dise.

But bargain hunting is more than just buying for less. It's also buying smart. When you know the secrets of successful bargain hunting, you also know—and practice—smart consumerism. You know how to evaluate products and services before you buy, so you get don't get roped into purchasing things you don't want and don't need that can potentially cost you more than just the purchase price in expensive or frequent repairs.

That means you save time, which in itself is a valuable commod-ity, as well as money. And remember, every dollar you save is an extra dollar in your bank account.

If you're an entrepreneur, as more and more of us are these days, bargain shopping makes your capital go farther, even when you have only a limited amount—especially important when you're starting a company. As a bargain hunter, you can make your business look like a million bucks on a shoestring budget.

Bargain hunting is easy—not an approach that takes years to perfect. People who've attended our talks and read our books tell us they saved money the very first time they used our techniques. (In fact, one lady who was self-professedly timid and shy negotiated her first bargain from *us*—during one of our bargain hunting and savvy consumer seminars!) If she can do it, you can too.

Twelve Secrets Of The Bargain Seeker

The world is brimming with bargains and places to find them. We'll explore them as we go through this book. But no matter where you go, whatever bargain you're hunting, you'll use the same set of tactics: the Twelve Secrets of the Bargain Seeker.

You don't have to spend hours memorizing these strategies or do all your shopping with your nose stuck in this book, anxiously thumbing through dog-eared pages. These secrets employ simple, common-sense techniques that will quickly become second-nature. They're civilized, courteous, and resourceful. And they'll take you everywhere you want to go, on every shopping adventure. Once you've mastered them, you can bargain with the best.

Ready? Here we go!

Secret 1: Don't be shy.

The bottom line—the basement—of bargaining is haggling, or, if you prefer, discussing the price: what the merchant is willing to take versus what you're willing to spend.

The word *bargain*, by way of Middle French and then English, stems from the ancient Latin term *"barcaniare"* for trade. And that's actually what bargaining is: a fair trade. You're trading your cash (or charge card) for the seller's products. But you're also trading in less tangible assets. You're giving the seller the opportunity to move merchandise— goods that cost him money sitting on the shelf—and you're giving him a valuable sales ally for the future—you!

continued on page 3

The average shopper is too faint-hearted to haggle. But most merchants, from superstore department managers to mom-and-pop operators, are surprisingly receptive.

Why? Merchants live in a store-eat-store world. They know that if you don't buy that product from them, you'll buy it from the competition. And they also know that if you walk out their doors, there's an excellent chance you won't come back. Therefore, they're motivated to sell to you while you're still a captive audience, and with good reason. Merchandise collecting dust on store shelves costs retailers money in more ways than one:

a) **Shoppers want to see and touch the latest model** and the latest fashion—in everything from clothing to carpets to commodes;

b) **Stock still on display leaves no room for the next generation** of product—the stuff that matches or beats the competition's merchandise;

c) **Merchandise still haunting the aisles** gives corporate office management the unpleasant idea that the store isn't generating much business.

So it's in the store manager's—and his department managers'—best interests to get rid of everything that's not fresh off the distributor's truck. The secret here is that merchants—no dummies—won't tell you they're anxious to see the last of this stuff. You have to nose around. You have to ask. And while there's no need to be bombastic, you certainly don't want to be shy. Remember that bargain hunting is an adventure!

Shelly peered at the jumble of glass. "I'd have to take $20 a box."

"You've got an awful lot of this stuff to get rid of," we countered. "How about $20 for both boxes?"

Shelly pursed her lips. "Well," she said reluctantly, "all right." We paid for our goodies and Shelly scurried back toward the warmth of the store.

Wow, we thought, we came out on top of that deal! The knobs would add just the right touch to a cottage we were renovating and we'd paid less than one-tenth of what they were worth.

But we weren't the only ones who made out like thieves. As we left the sale, we caught sight of Shelly exchanging high fives with a co-worker. "You know those old boxes of doorknobs?" she was crowing. "I finally got rid of them!"

Secret 2: Present a logical reason for the seller to discount.

Despite the fact that retailers are secretly anxious to sell, they're not simply going to hand over the store. You have to give them a reason or incentive to discount to you. Sometimes it's cash. Sometimes it's buying all they have of a certain item. Sometimes it's just the fact—to paraphrase Arnold Schwarzenegger—that you'll be back. Get creative. If you can't think of a reason, make one up. If nothing else, you'll get a good chuckle—and hopefully, so will the seller.

Here are the quintessential bargain hunter's reasons to discount, followed by a sample "icebreaker." You can use the lines as given or ad lib in whatever way suits the situation and your personality:

* **Overstocks.** *"I see you're a little overstocked here on the whatsits. How much would you discount one of them? What if I bought them all?"*

* **Overabundance of floor models.** *"I notice you have two floor models. How would you feel about discounting one, and I'll buy it?"* OR *"Say, what about that whosit over there that's not in a box? How much would you take for it?"*

* **Merchandise that's perfectly good but, because it was a display** or fell prey to some previous shopper's curiosity, is missing the original packaging. *"Say, what about that whosit over there that's not in a box? How much would you take for it?"*

* **Merchandise that's not quite perfect.** *"This television has a scratch along the side. How*

much can you give me off on it?" (No need to mention that you plan to put the TV in an entertainment center where the entire scratched side will be hidden from view.)

* **Not the newest model.** *"This computer is a 2 Ghz system, and all the new ones are faster and have larger hard drives. What's the best you can do for me on it?"*

* **Not the right season.** *"The weather's getting awfully cold for barbecuing and I see that's your last gas grill. Can you lower the price on it?"*

* **Cash.** This works better with small business retailers or private-party transactions than with chain stores that have to report to somebody else. The attraction for the independent seller is that he doesn't have to worry that your check might bounce, he doesn't have to wait for it to clear, and he doesn't have to pay the extra percentage charged him by credit card companies. *"I see you're asking $50 for that do-hickey. Could you take $40 for it if I paid cash?"*

* **You'll be back to buy more.** *"In my whatever business, I always need whatsits. If you can get the price down for me, I'll be in here a lot to buy more."*

We wanted that vanity. The damaged side could be removed, since it would sit flush against our bathroom wall, and all the kick plate needed was to be reattached with a couple of screws. But it wasn't a bargain. Yet.

The next week the vanity had been reduced an additional $100—now it was going for half price. OK! we thought. It was unlikely at this point that anyone else would want a dented 5-foot cabinet. We approached Clint, the department manager, and offered him $40—one-tenth of the original price.

Clint suggested we come back on Friday, when he'd know his profit margin for the week. It must have been a good one, because when we returned Friday afternoon he flashed us a grin and said, "Get that thing out of here."

We did. And it looked terrific.

[If you don't have a reason, make one up.]

Secret 3: Don't get attached. Or at least don't show it.

This secret's often the most difficult to adhere to. It can also be the most important. Whatever it is you want to buy, don't want it so badly that you lose your ability to bargain. Once the seller sees that you must have his product, he knows he's got you hooked and he loses his incentive to come down in price.

So dull that gleam in your eye. Even though that whatsit might be exactly what you want in every way, shape, and form, act nonchalant. If the salesman asks why you're drooling, say you haven't had lunch yet.

If you know yourself, and you know you'll have a hard time not waxing rhapsodic over whatsits, bring a friend. Study old *Law and Order* episodes and perform the bargain-hunting version of good cop/bad cop.

Let's say you're shopping for a sofa, for example, and you find one you adore. You blurt out that the color is perfect for your living room. The salesman gets excited—he smells a sale. Your partner counters that the sofa might be too big for your space. The salesman, fearing a lost commission, swings into negotiating mode.

But you're still blinded by love. You exclaim that the sofa's classic lines match the rest of your décor and your dog will like the cushy pillows. The salesman gets excited again. Your bad cop partner immediately points out that it's more money than you had planned on spending. And the salesman goes back on bargain alert.

After your friend kicks you in the shin, you wise up and get with the program. You walk away and look at something less expensive. "Well," you say, "if that first sofa we looked at was priced like this one, I might go for it." You still want the one with the cushy pillows, but you don't show it. And you let the bargaining begin.

Expedition Tip

When a product is marked at 50 percent (or whatever percent) off, check the tag for the base price. By law, merchants must specify this base price so you can figure the bottom line for yourself.

Don't be fooled by stores that run perpetual going-out-of-business sales. This is your clue that they've grossly overpriced their merchandise so they can "mark it down" for unwary shoppers. In many areas, in fact, you need a license to run a going-out-of-business sale. Ask your local Better Business Bureau if your area is one of these. If so, there's a good chance the sale is legitimate.

Secret 4: Make buddies, and make yourself available.

Get to know the folks who run the stores you frequent. As you cruise the aisles, keep your eyes open for familiar faces. Find out who's who: the department managers, the store manager, the sharpest associates. They're the ones who know what's really going on in the store—what and where the bargains are. And they're the ones who either have the power to discount or the ambition to take your discount request to someone who can approve it.

These salespeople are not store servants—they're potential allies. Find out their names and then ask for them the next time you come in. This secret has an additional bonus: You develop a rapport with the salesperson you've asked for, but you also begin a rapport with his or her co-workers. They'll notice that you're asking for So-and-so and will make it their business to find out why. And when they discover you're a good customer for their own department's special sales, they'll call you.

Reward your store allies. Many stores reward employees who provide good customer service. When one of your sources gives you a good deal, call or write to the store manager and tell him how much you appreciate So-and-so's service and extra attention. Besides being a nice gesture, it gives your buddy one more reason to remember you when the next special mark-down comes around.

The face that launches a thousand deals: Once you've established yourself as a bargain hunter with your sales allies, the very sight of you in the store will often set visions of special sale items (or as we call them, "must-goes") dancing through their heads—special items that they'll pass on to you.

Secret 5: You gotta shop around.

You can't know what a good deal is until you know what it isn't. Be your own *Consumer Reports*. Get out there and investigate whatever it is you want to buy. Explore as many makes and models as possible, especially when hunting big-ticket items. Decide which features are on your must-have list and which you can live without. At the same time, compare prices between models and between stores. Find out when the next generation, or next model, is expected out, because that's when prices on the current models will drop—sometimes drastically.

Don't dump everything and decide you've got to have a new freezer *today,* unless it's August and ice cream is puddling into lakes at the bottom of your current model. You'll do much better when you give yourself time to shop around. Instead of pressuring yourself or your significant other to make that buying decision immediately, make your rounds.

Visit your sales allies and put them on the lookout for your dream whatsit. At the same time, stroll down other avenues—stores you haven't previously visited, catalogs, and the Internet. Then when you track down that terrific bargain, you'll *know* it's a great deal.

> [You can't know what a good deal is until you know what it isn't.]

Build a finders network that provides you with insider tips to save money. Tell your contacts—the people who make up your network of vendors, suppliers, contractors, and acquaintances—that you'll pay a finder's fee when they tell you of a deal in your field.

If you're a landscape contractor, for instance, you might ask for tips on mature trees and shrubs being uprooted to make way for new building. Then pick these up for a song (with permission from the owner first) and sell them to your customers.

If you invest in real estate or are in the market for new business quarters, ask for tips on properties that are about to—but haven't yet—come on the market. Then get ready for tips from such seemingly unlikely sources as appliance repairmen, pest control technicians, and house painters.

Secret 6: Show that your intentions are serious.

Sellers are much more interested in buyers than in looky-loos, and therefore, they're more motivated to bargain. So once again, get out there and get nosy. Ask questions about the product. Demonstrate the research you've already done. If, for example, you're hunting a dishwasher, ask about features like cycles, noise level, water usage, and rust-free interior parts.

This tells the salesperson that you know what you want, you're informed about the merchandise—possibly because you've just come from the competition down the street—and you're serious about buying. It motivates him to take you seriously, and to take your bargain-seeking seriously as well. He doesn't want you taking your brilliance—and your bucks—somewhere else.

Once you've made that purchase, remember that you've also made a friend in the business. Seek out your new buddy the next time you're in the store. Let him know how much you're enjoying your whatsit and how much you appreciate the deal he gave you.

And every time you're in the store, even if you don't need anything in that department, stop in and say, as Gomer Pyle would, a friendly "Hey!" Ask if anything special is coming up. Keep the lines of communication open.

Expedition Tip

Before you buy either on the Net or at brick-and-mortar stores, use online comparison shopping sites like CNET.com, mySimon.com, and ConsumerSearch.com to research prices and features.

BUSINESS BEACON
Delegating Authority

Running a business—especially a new one—is like child care. It demands a lot of time, energy, and attention. But it needn't stop you from being a smart consumer and bargain hunter. If you don't have time to research the products or services you need to buy, assign the task to an employee. Or, if you *are* the employee in your SOHO (small office/home office) company, assign the job to a family member who likes to shop or is a Web-surfing and researching whiz.

Secret 7: Be willing to walk away.

If the seller doesn't accept your offer and won't compromise, walk away. Sometimes this is what it takes to get that great deal. As the old cliché goes, the grass is always greener on the other side—the other side being your retreating backside. Once the seller sees you heading into the sunset, he's often already wishing he'd changed his mind. And if you walk slowly enough, he often will.

Secret 8: Be willing to walk back.

Sometimes you have to walk back. Give the seller a chance to change his mind. You're not losing face; you're keeping negotiations open. And you're showing the seller you think enough of him and his product to want to return. Think back to your own experiences in selling a car or a house. Haven't there been times when you wished you hadn't been so quick to turn down an offer? Wished the potential buyer would walk back through your door? Well, here's your opportunity to make someone else's dream come true.

Sometimes, one more day of sitting on a piece of merchandise that hasn't sold is enough to get the seller to rethink your offer. Sometimes it's a few days or even a month. Occasionally, it can be a matter of moments.

We walked into our local home improvement superstore one sunny Sunday afternoon to buy a garden hose. We came out with a 31-inch TV that we got for about half price. The TV was a floor model, the store was about to close down to move to a new location, and the department manager was not looking forward to lugging the thing across town. He'd already marked it down to $600 from the regular retail price of $800.

We offered $350. Bud, the manager, shook his head. "If I sold it to you for that price," he said, "I'd have half the employees in here trying to kill me because I didn't offer it to them first." Then he gave the TV another glance. He really didn't want the dang thing. "OK," he said finally, "I'll give it to you for $450."

Bud said that was the best he could do. Unfortunately, it was more than we wanted to spend. And since we hadn't come into the store for a TV in the first place, we thanked him for his time, took our garden hose, and walked out. Halfway through the parking lot, we had a brainstorm.

We ditched the hose in the car, scuttled back into the store and offered Bud his $450—if he could include the tax in that price. Bud got out his calculator, reverse-engineered a sale price of about $420, and we went home with a new TV.

Expedition Tip

Take the peaks and valleys of the salesperson's day into consideration when you're bargaining. If it's a hectic Saturday afternoon and he's surrounded by shoppers demanding his attention, let him know *briefly* what you're interested in and come back another day. He'll appreciate you for it—and you'll get a better deal.

Secret 9: Don't insult and don't get insulted.

Rob once got thrown out of a junkyard for insulting the merchandise. (Actually it wasn't him; it was the friend he was with, whose negotiating skills left a great deal to be desired). Rob knows: Bargaining is a friendly process. It's sounding out the seller and letting him sound you out. Once you get a sense of where each of you is coming from—and trying to go—you can make your offer. It can be a shade shy of the marked price, or it can be ridiculously low.

But it should never, ever be offered in an insulting manner. That's not the way to win friends or influence people. No one is going to cut you a better deal because you offended him. No one is going to welcome you back or call you with a special deal because you scorned his wares.

If you suggest a discount on the grounds that a product is flawed, don't ever say something like, "How much would you take for that ratty old dresser with the missing drawer pulls?" Even in a second-hand store, you're insulting the seller. Instead, you'll want to word it along the lines of, "This is a great dresser, but the drawer pulls are missing. It's going to cost me **X** dollars to replace them. Can you give me **Y** off the price?"

While you're taking care not to insult the seller, make sure that you don't get *your* feelings hurt, either. Eventually, you're going to catch somebody on a day when everything's gone wrong and your bargain offer comes as the straw that breaks the seller's back. Don't take it personally. Chances are that the next time you encounter that seller, he'll be delighted to work with you.

[When you know the markup, you have a handle on the merchant's cost.]

The Magic Mark-Up

There is no one magic mark-up for any retail or wholesale sector, no single percentage you can figure into every deal. It all depends on what the merchant paid for his goods and the savings he wants to pass along to the average customer.

But there are industry norms, mark-ups that more or less hold true across the board. Oriental rug dealers, for instance, mark up their merchandise so that after they give you a 50 percent discount, they still have between 30 percent and 50 percent profit left in the piece. Standard-model major appliances, on the other hand, typically are marked up only about 15 percent. But deluxe models—like that refrigerator with the icemaker, water dispenser, and mood lighting in the door— carry higher mark-ups of up to 30 percent.

continued on page 13

Secret 10: Find out the seller's mark-up.

As you make friends in the merchants' world, start nosing out mark-ups—the difference between what the product is selling for and what the merchant paid for it. The reason? Unless it's one of those discount-or-die situations, the seller isn't likely to let go of his merchandise for less than his cost. Knowing the mark-up gives you a handle on how much bargaining room you've got—and gives you that bargain-hunter's rush when you come across a really great deal.

Electronics and small appliances like microwaves and toasters also get marked up about 30 percent, while knick-knacks and giftwares can zoom up 150 percent. If you want to sit down and mull this over, you'll do so on furniture that carries a 55 percent mark-up, the same amount as toys.

You can check out some typical mark-ups in the sidebar on pages 12 and 13, but keep in mind that the ones your sales buddies are working with will vary depending on many factors, including the kind of deal they got for the goods. And the mark-ups for private-party merchandise can veer all over the place. That's why it's important for you to do your own research.

Again, don't worry about being nosy. Most people appreciate a healthy interest, especially when they see that you're working toward making an offer.

Some typical icebreakers:

* *What's the store's cost for whosits?*
* *This is terrific old whatsit. Do you remember what you paid for it?*
* *I understand there's not a lot of mark-up on do-hickeys. What's your profit margin?*

Treasure Chest Trivia

If you're between the ages of 45 and 54, get ready to be depressed: You spend more money on just about every type of purchase than any other age group, according to the U.S. Bureau of Labor Statistics.

Secret 11: Strike when the deal is hot.

This one is the reverse face of the "Shop Around" secret. Doing your research before you buy is excellent strategy, but every once in a while a really fabulous deal comes up—usually when you least expect it—and bites you in the backside. When that happens, you've got to be ready to jump—as in the case where we went into the store for a garden hose and came out with a television.

We weren't looking for a TV at the time, but because we'd nosed around the electronics departments a lot just for fun (and researching while we were at it), we recognized the TV as a terrific bargain. And we knew our old set was about ready for the Great Electronic Afterlife. So when the deal jumped up and bit us, we bit back. If we'd waited until our old set coughed out its last commercial, the Terrific TV would have been long gone, snapped up by some other savvy shopper or a store employee.

This is not to advise, of course, that you should run around town with your money burning a hole in your back pocket, ready to spend it on every piece of merchandise that makes eyes at you. Savvy bargain seekers are shopping adventurers, but they're responsible, informed ones. Some deals you just have to let slip through your fingers. No bargain is terrific for you if it puts a strain on your budget or you just don't need it.

BARGAIN HUNTER'S JOURNAL
Hang Onto That Hall Tree

When Judy Casey was a young married in Savannah, Georgia, her husband suggested they go look at an antique brass bed that he'd seen advertised in the local paper. Judy felt that a furniture purchase would seriously dent their budget, but since her husband really wanted a brass bed, she agreed to go look. The first thing she saw when they walked in the door of the old house was a beautiful oak-and-brass hall tree.

"I fell in love with that hall tree," Judy says. "My heart was beating so fast I was afraid the elderly lady who owned the house would see it practically pounding out of my chest. But I didn't even know if it was for sale."

Then Judy fell for an oak armoire and a gorgeous carved oak complete bedroom set.

continued on page 15

Look at the unattainable deal this way. If it doesn't fit your pocketbook now, another one (maybe even better!) will show up later—after you've smartly saved your pennies on more affordable bargains. And in the meantime, like a die-hard fisherman, you can recount stories of "the one that got away."

Secret 12: Let in a little serendipity.

One of the really keen aspects of bargain hunting is that, after a while, bargains seem to find you. You get a reputation for having that magic touch, the one that attracts unbelievable deals and incites a healthy envy among your peers. It *is* magic—and it stems from your ability to see every shopping experience as a potential bargain and to recognize the truly outstanding ones when they come along. It also has something to do with your sense of adventure. Bargain hunting, like life, presents a lot of unexpected dividends when you open yourself up to them.

The savvy bargain seeker leaves plenty of room for serendipity. Keep your eyes and ears open, your sense of humor honed, and your bargaining antennae tuned, and you'll find those terrific deals in even the most unexpected places.

[After a while, bargains seem to find you.]

All dutiful intentions of budgeting flew out the window on the Savannah breeze. She knew she was looking at the real thing: antiques that had the patina only time, classic craftsmanship, and a century of care can give to furniture. And she knew that this was a one-in-a-million opportunity. The seller was anxious to get rid of everything and Judy realized that the more she bought, the better price she'd get. She told her husband he could have the brass bed if the woman would sell the other pieces— including the hall tree— as well.

The woman was delighted to oblige. Judy got all the antiques, including the hall tree, with a loan she arranged through her credit union. She's long since paid off the loan, but the antiques are still treasures in her home. She's frequently asked to sell the hall tree—the last offer was for $2,000. Even though she paid only $50 for it, she says, "I wouldn't sell it for anything. It's priceless to me."

Shopping Therapy

Bargain hunting is not only good for your bottom line, it's also good therapy. You can't make a mistake, you can't make a fool of yourself, and you won't hurt anybody's feelings. What you can do is get in the spirit of getting out, getting involved, and making friends in the business of wherever you're shopping.

This is particularly good for SOHO (small office/home office) entrepreneurs. When you work at home—and especially alone—you can feel isolated and even a little stir-crazy. Shopping the bargain hunter's way encourages you to get away from your desk for a while and out into the mainstream. It's networking with an edge.

Chapter Two
Hidden Treasure

Now that you've read this far, you know that retail stores have a lot more for sale than what you see on the display floor. And you know that just because the shop doesn't have a big sign in the window that says "Sale" doesn't mean there isn't anything *on* sale. But did you know that the very best buys, the ones that make the bargain hunter's heart soar, aren't advertised inside the store either?

It's true. The best stuff isn't advertised in the newspaper, it doesn't carry a sale sticker, and it may not even be out among the merchandise. Follow along with us in this chapter as we unlock the hidden treasures behind the Retail Veil.

Unadvertised Loot

Stores often have perfectly good merchandise that they want to move but haven't promoted, either because the advertised sale won't start for several days or because they only have a few of each item. You'll find these gems stacked in the aisle, crowded near the front door, or even at the curb. Sometimes they're simply tucked on the shelf with a discreet mark-down sticker attached.

Well, we hear you asking, if all those things are overflowing into the aisles or falling out the front door, how come nobody knows they're on sale? The answer, dear reader, is that most people aren't bargain hunters. They perceive that jumble of products as just that—a jumble.

They never take a second glance. It doesn't occur to them to ask what all that stuff is. You, as a bargain hunter, will of course do just that. And you'll learn that it's a) merchandise that's just now being tagged for an upcoming sale, b) merchandise that's being taken off the shelves because it didn't sell, or c) brand-new products that have just come in and haven't yet been put on the shelves.

If the answer is *a*, you're in the right place at the right time! You can have your pick today of whatever will be tomorrow's store special. If it's *b*, you're still in the right place because now's your chance to make that can't-be-refused offer. The manager will often take less than what the store originally paid just to get the goods off his books. And if it's *c*, you got the thrill of asking—and you've made another contact with the store personnel.

Treasure Chest Trivia

Americans are big spenders when it comes to retail sales, buying roughly $3.2 trillion worth of goods in a single year, according to a recent report by the National Retail Federation.

Sticker Mania

What about the merchandise that's already got a sale sticker on it? You can negotiate for it too, so don't take that sticker as the final price. You can tell if the product has been on the shelf for a while, either by checking on it every time you come into the store or by the amount of dust that may have accumulated on its surface. When you find an item that hasn't moved in weeks bring it to the department manager and ask if he'll take less. You'll be surprised at how often the answer is yes. If it's no, ask if it might come down in price later. Even if the answer is still no, ask again the next time you come in and the next (providing of course that you don't ask every day—your objective here is not to drive them insane).

What *is* your objective? To remind the department manager that the thing is wasting space on the shelf and that he's got a willing buyer in you. And sooner or later, he'll probably give you a steal of a deal on it.

Expedition Tip

What you see on clearance sale mark-down tables is often the tip of the iceberg. Check back every few days for new additions and price reductions. Go again at the end of the last day of the sale for the ultimate in mark-down bargaining.

The Riches In The Back Room

If you could take a peek into the store's back room, you'd see all sorts of one-of-a-kind goodies tucked away—merchandise that's perfectly good, or even brand-new, but can't be sold as new. Sometimes these items are displays, a television or refrigerator or even a table that's been out on the floor for customers to view. They look sharp, have never been used, and may not even have been plugged in. But what happens when a newer model comes along or when that particular version goes out of stock?

The store has to get rid of the old model, even though there's absolutely nothing wrong with it. And since that display's been out in the public eye for several weeks or months, it can't be called new. The original packaging has usually long since disappeared, and often the handy booklet that gives all those cautions about not using electronic devices underwater or sticking your hair into moving parts—and describes how to program the thing—has disappeared as well. But the savvy bargain hunter takes this as a challenge instead of a negative.

We bought a brand-new Whirlpool electric range that originally sold for $450 for $150. It wasn't in a box, but that was good—less cardboard to break down and throw away. It didn't come with the instruction booklet, but that was okay—we could figure out how to turn it on. We loaded it onto the back of our pick-up truck and drove away. Once in our kitchen, we set it up, plugged it in, and proudly popped in a casserole. And listened to it beep—and beep and beep. Apparently it wanted something, but without any instructions, who knew?

Well, we'd been through this type of thing before. We have a $200 cordless telephone/answering machine that we bought for $25. It works great, but it took us a month to figure out how to program the time. Until then, we never knew when people had called. The thing would announce that the message had been taken on Wednesday at 3:10 in the morning when in actuality it had been on Sunday at 4:00 in the afternoon.

But back to the oven. After we experimentally punched a few buttons, we discovered that all it wanted was for us to press *Start*. And programming the time was easy—all we had to do was hit the clock key, set the time, and hit clock again. If you know how one set of electronic gizmos "thinks," you can generally figure out the next.

And if you're just not mechanically (or electronically) minded—you're one of those people who *still* hasn't figured out how to set the VCR even though you've got every piece of paper it came with—not to worry. The manufacturer will usually cheerfully send you an instruction pamphlet—all you have to do is call and request it.

Expedition Tip

Don't panic if the TV remote has disappeared along with the packaging. If the TV you bought, for instance, is an RCA, look for an RCA universal remote, which you can purchase for around $10 at any Wal-Mart-type superstore or electronics retailer. Chances are its default setting will work your TV without any programming on your part.

Manhandled By Mechanics

Another goody in the back room's secret cache is the demo. This is usually some piece of electronic equipment—a TV, stereo system, or computer that's been out on the display floor broadcasting Oprah or the local country western radio station or running a looped multimedia commercial about the computer's capabilities. And because it's been doing so for months, it can't be called new.

Some demos still have that fresh-out-of-the-box look. Others have obviously been well used—you'll see fingerprints that sometimes make them look like they've been manhandled by a gang of auto mechanics at their grimiest, and mucky, sticky patches where various stickers have been applied and then inexpertly peeled off.

Most people would never dream of purchasing a sullied piece of electronic equipment, reasoning that if it looks dirty it must be beat up—inside and out. Not! These beauty defects are usually only skin deep. A little cleaning solution and that unattractive piece of equipment will sparkle like new. And run great. Electronics nowadays are designed to last, so a TV or CD player that's been up and running for a year is still a relative infant. And if it's been operating for that long, you can assume it doesn't have any bugs.

Computer Demo Crash Course

A computer is a major purchase—one that's going to help you run your home or office and possibly your life. Follow these tips to determine whether that darling demo is a deal or a dud:

* **Find out how long it's been a demo.** This will give you an idea of how state-of-the-art it is, whether it has the latest bells and whistles or is already an antique. (If it's more than a year old, you may want to look elsewhere.)
* **Examine it for possible flaws.** Test the keyboard. Are there sticky or nonfunctioning keys? Do the monitor's contrast and bright dials work? You can sometimes negotiate a new keyboard into the deal.
* **Ask the store manager to get you past the demo loop into the system so you can test the software.** (Make sure she removes the lock-out that keeps that loop running before you leave the store with your new purchase.)
* **Make sure the other accessories,** microphone, speakers, mouse and cords, are present and accounted for.
* **Make sure you get the CD-ROMS for all pre-installed software**—especially Windows or other operating systems. Without them you can't restore the system if you have a problem. If they can't find the CDs, ask for an additional discount to make up for the programs you'll have to buy. (You can also call the manufacturer and have them send you a software package.)
* **Ask for the full warranty.**
* **And that's it.** Take that baby home and have fun with it!

But remember: Don't get your feelings hurt if a brand-new upgraded model comes out a week later. You got a great deal because yours was being retired. And the newest model isn't always the best. Be happy with your proven all-star and let somebody else work the bugs out of the new one.

In The Eye Of The Beholder

It's not easy being a retailer. They often get stuck with merchandise that's been damaged in their own warehouses or on the delivery truck. Stock clerks have little accidents with that forklift, or they load their trucks like Fibber McGee's closet—when it gets to the store and the doors are opened, *bloomph!* Everything comes crashing out onto the unloading area's concrete floor. In clothing stores customers who are a size 14 insist on trying that size 10 dress—instant ripped seam.

This is not a bad thing for the bargain hunter. Most buyers see beauty only in a flawless product. But to the bargain hunter, damaged goods are gorgeous—and another win/win situation for you and the merchant. A lot of damage is not as bad as it may look at first glance. Or it takes less to repair than what you might imagine. And very often the manufacturer will send you replacement parts at no charge.

We bought a $300 GE dishwasher with a dented face panel for $225. It was the last one on the floor, the last year's model, and it was damaged, so the department manager was more than happy to negotiate. We called the manufacturer, explaining that we'd purchased a damaged product and we wanted a replacement panel. A week later the UPS man delivered a brand-new one to our door. Total installation time: five minutes. New look: perfect. Price: 25 percent off retail.

We also picked up a really snazzy $200 Hollywood-style oak medicine cabinet with tri-fold mirrored doors for $50. The only problem was that the mirrors were cracked. (We didn't do it, so we weren't worried about bad luck.) We carted the thing home in its opened box, propped it up in the hallway and called the manufacturer. In a few days the company sent us a new set of doors. Installation time: half hour. New look: stunning. Price: 75 percent off retail.

Expedition Tip

Don't forget that every piece of dinged or dented merchandise you rescue is one item that doesn't go to the landfill. Which makes you environmentally aware and ecologically friendly—a green, whole-earth good guy or gal!

Enlisted As An Ally

How do you nose out these terrific deals? Take a spin around the store. Chances are you'll see a refrigerator with a crunch on one side (forklift accident), an oven with a smushed door (fell out of the truck), or a washer or dryer with scratches along the side (shopping carts taking those corners too tight).

Be a snoop shopper. Peer into every nook and cranny of the department you want. That damaged item will generally be tucked discreetly to one side—and you'll be surprised at how often the very thing you're looking for is just around the corner. Even if it's already got a sale tag on it, ask the department manager if he can do better. One of his jobs is to get rid of unsightly merchandise, and he'll be delighted to enlist you as an ally.

Sometimes you find a damaged snazzola-model product that's been marked down, but it's still pricey. How do you get the manager to reduce the price still further? By explaining your options and asking for his help. Try something like this:

> **You:** *I'm interested in this dishwasher with the dented face plate, but it's awfully expensive considering it's been damaged. I can buy a brand-new bottom of the line model in perfect condition for less than this one here. Can you come down on it?*
>
> **Department Manager:** *Well, I could reduce it another $25.*
>
> **You:** *I'd appreciate that, but it still makes it more expensive than this cheaper model. Can you at least match the bottom-of-the-line price?*
>
> **Department Manager:** *Hmm. I'd have to check the computer and see what our profit margin is on it. (checks computer) I could come down another $50.*
>
> **You:** *Thank you!*

Treasure Chest Trivia

Furniture retailers have a higher profit margin—that is, they make more money—on upholstered furniture than on *case goods*, the wooden pieces like tables and desks. Why? Case goods tend to get dinged up en route to the warehouse or the customer's home and the retailer has to pay to have them detailed and repaired. But nice, cushy upholstered pieces don't get damaged—hence they cost the retailer less money.

Damage Assessment

One of the delights of bargain hunting is getting creative—figuring out how to restore, replace, or otherwise compensate for terrific products the average shopper sees only as damaged goods.

You can hide a flaw, ask the manufacturer to replace a defective part, or restore an item to like-new condition with paint, needle and thread, or elbow grease.

But if that damaged item doesn't come with a warranty and it isn't working at all (meaning you have no clue what the problem could be), you're gambling. Often the store will take as much as 90 percent off as an incentive for you to take it away. (They're as much in the dark as you are.)

But this is like buying a lottery ticket. The problem can be as a simple as a blown fuse on a television or as major as a compressor on a refrigerator, which has now become a storage cabinet—at least until you make a deal with a repair technician for a new compressor.

[One of the delights of bargain hunting is getting creative—turning a seemingly damaged product into a treasure.]

continued on page 25

Right As Rain

Sometimes the only damage is to the packaging. Heavy, bulky items like assemble-it-yourself furniture, closet organizers, and weight sets frequently suffer packaging woes.

If the cardboard's gotten wet or opened and re-taped a dozen times, it's liable to look pretty grim—and the store knows no one will pay full price for it, even though what's inside is right as rain. Sometimes the store will reduce it to cost to get rid of it. If it's been around a very long time or is the last one of a close-out, they'll reduce it even further.

Instead we called the manufacturer, who cheerfully took our purchase information, gave us a three-year warranty, and offered to send out either a technician or a replacement machine. We opted for the machine. They shipped it immediately and it's been running happily for years.

Peek inside and if you think it's okay, go for it—but try for a guarantee that if it's missing parts you can bring it back. If you can't, make sure they reduce the price enough to make it worth your while.

Return To Sender

You'd be astonished at the kinds of things people purchase and then take back to the store. We've seen major appliances that have been used—and in some cases used hard—and returned. Airless sprayers to hot tubs to small appliances, you name it and it's been brought back. Then there's that clothing with the seam ripped out (buyer heavier than anticipated) or with lipstick on the collar. Sometimes it seems fairly obvious that customers purchase products as a sort of short-term rental, then take them back when they're finished with them.

Why does the store cheerfully refund their money? Sometimes the merchant has a satisfaction-guaranteed policy, sometimes the management believes it's better to mollify a customer than lose him along with possible future sales, and sometimes the customer is just pushy enough to get away with it.

All this is terrific for you, the bargain hunter. Sometimes there's nothing at all wrong with the merchandise, but it's marked down because it's been returned. Electronic equipment—from TVs to VCRs to CD players—frequently gets brought back because the customer insists it doesn't work. If you can buy it for the right price, it pays to take a chance and take it home. Often you'll discover that the only thing that doesn't work is the previous owners' mechanical aptitude. Either they didn't have it hooked up right or they couldn't figure out how to program it.

People will also return partially-assembled build-it-yourself furniture because halfway through the project they discovered the "simple" instructions were beyond them. If you're not do-it-yourself (DIY)-challenged you can pick these things up at store cost, bring them home and easily reassemble them.

Sometimes that returned item does need repair, but the problem is so minor that you can either easily fix it yourself or have a specialist do it for relative pennies.

Terry bought a $65 pair of jeans at a trendy boutique for $9 because the zipper was broken. How could she resist? A 10-minute trip to the seamstress cost another $5. End result: a fashionable garment for less than 75 percent of the marked price.

Expedition Tip

Mend a weak leg on a table or chair by wrapping a piece of tin around it and then gluing it in place. The tin adds strength and can easily be bent to conform to odd shapes.

BARGAIN HUNTER'S JOURNAL
In The Right Place

Vernon Heywood of Corona, California brought home a gorgeous Craftsman-style sofa from an upscale home furnishings store for 50 percent off retail. The only thing wrong with it: the customer who ordered it custom-upholstered didn't like the finished product once she saw it.

So the store was stuck with it—and quite a few more custom-ordered and rejected pieces as well. Its solution: hold a liquidation clearance sale.

Vern was in the right place at the right time— he managed the store. But any bargain hunter can get the same sort of deal. Just walk into a similar store—if there isn't a sale going on, ask if they have any returns.

Tool Time

So you're planning to shop for those abused items and restore them to glory. Terrific! You're in for a lot of fun, the glow of accomplishment, and the pride that comes with doing-it-yourself (and showing off your great deals).

Now, what tools do you need to have on hand to work your restoration wiles? Here's a handy checklist of the essential items that should be in every treasure-seeking bargain hunter's workspace. (If you don't have them all, that's OK—you can put them on your track-down list):

Hand tools:
- Hammer
- Screwdriver
- Pliers
- Channel-locks
- Adjustable or crescent wrench
- Tin snips
- Small carpenter's square
- Set of wood chisels
- Heavy-duty stapler

Power tools:
- Drill (cordless or corded)
- Jigsaw
- Circular saw
- Electric miter box
- Hot glue gun

The Last of Its Kind

We've discussed all sorts of goodies that you can find because they have some sort of flaw, whether real or perceived. But did you know that you can also negotiate great bargains on brand-new merchandise? Really!

This is wonderful stuff that the retailer is no longer motivated to sell because they're never going to carry it again. Rob once bought a $3,400 leather sofa for $800 because the store was shutting down its furniture department.

Retailers will sometimes advertise these kinds of bargains, along with the ever-popular going-out-of-business sale. But just because it's in the paper doesn't mean you can't negotiate an even better deal.

The Pleasures Of Price Matching

They won't often tell you unless you ask, but many stores have a hard-to-beat Beat the Competition policy. If you find the same item with a better price at another retailer, they'll not only match that price, but knock off 10 percent of the difference.

In our business of renovating beach properties, we're always running to the home improvement store for drywall, lumber, and other construction materials. And if you've ever done any building or remodeling, you know that these things don't come cheap.

So we make a practice of calling to check prices at a couple different stores before we leave home. Frequently one will come up a dollar or so cheaper than another. We head for the more expensive store (which is usually the best one in town and the one where we do most of our business), tell them that their competitor down the road is selling drywall for $1 less (or whatever), and place our order. The savings add up quickly.

The store's not sorry we're doing this—in fact, they like it. Why? Because they know (and they're right) that while we're there, taking advantage of the savings on drywall, we're also loading up our shopping cart with all sorts of other materials. And they're delighted that we're buying this stuff from them and not from their competitor.

If you don't know whether the store has a price-matching policy, ask. Here's a sample of what to say and how to say it:

* **Computer Caramba** *is selling the same model monitor that you have marked at $350 for $300. Can you match it?*

* **Barb's Boutique** *has this exact Pucci leather bomber jacket for $80 and yours is marked at $100. Do you think you could bring your price down?*

Now, when you're trying for price-matching, it's important to make sure both stores have exactly the same item. If it's a different brand or a different model, it won't work.

continued on page 30

Sometimes manufacturers will build in slight differences in the same products and give them different model numbers, just to save store chains from having to price-match. For instance, a range built for one appliance retailer will have the little green or red light that tells you the oven's on placed on the right, while the same range designed for another giant appliance chain will have the little light on the left. Sometimes the knobs will be a different color. Different model number, different specs. So no price-matching. But fortunately for the bargain hunter, this isn't always the case.

Keep in mind, however, that not all stores have a price-matching policy. If they don't, you can buy that item anyway—or smile, thank them for considering your request, and walk away. Part of the fun of bargain hunting is the thrill of the chase—but it doesn't mean you're going to land every deal you go after. And if you treat that manager with respect and with a sense of humor, he'll remember you the next time. And he just might come up with a bargain.

blends at a discount, and the dessert vendor suggests and then delivers the latest chocoholics' delight at a discounted price.

How did all this come about? Our friend discovered—through an employee with a bubbly personality who befriends everyone who walks in the door—that treating these vendors as friends instead of walking invoices paid off royally.

When these suppliers come by now, the owner greets them warmly and asks their advice about what's new and exciting in the market. She expresses interest in their wares and she asks for—and gets—great discounts.

The Affair Of The Off-Season Shopper

Terrific bargains sometimes start with an already-on-sale price—merchandise that's marked down because its time is past, like Christmas trimmings in January. But not all sales come post-season—stores often push pre-season goods to get shoppers in the mood and spending. There's a time and a season for every product under heaven, and as a savvy bargain hunter, you should know what they are. Follow along as we take a virtual spin through the retail sales year, alighting at each red-alert shopping event.

     The Bargain Hunter's [& Smart Consumer's] Field Guide

January. With the big holiday extravaganza behind them, stores are anxious to see the last of just about everything they brought in for the season—which means major mark-downs on all sorts of stuff. Look for sales on tools for Dad, sporting goods for Junior, holiday gift-boxed goodies like perfume and bath sets, chocolates, gourmet food baskets, and of course, clothing.

February. Home in on home furnishings and décor, including everyday dishes and dinnerware, because stores have an overflow of overstocks and returns on hand from the holidays. Add in the fact that this is the slowest month for this market and you've got a recipe for great deals. This is also a terrific time to shop for whatever lawn and garden items are left from last season before retailers bring in new merchandise for spring. And before we leave February, don't forget to look out for Valentine's Day sales and for mark-downs afterwards. Save all those heart-shaped chocolates and heart-sprinkled undies for later love tokens—or eat or wear them now!

Expedition Tip

While you can easily find boxes of Christmas cards for weeks after the holidays, stores clear out individual cards for lesser holidays like Valentine's Day, Mother's Day, and Easter immediately after the big event. So if you want to stock up for next year, you'll have to move fast.

March. It's spring cleaning time for many major chains, which means aisles of marked-down merchandise to be replaced with new stock. Spring—along with fall—is also when new computer models arrive on the scene, so it's the perfect time to make a deal on those suddenly outmoded units that still work great. Hop into pre-holiday sales on Easter bonnets and Easter decorations. And get in the green with St. Paddy's Day sales, too.

Expedition Tip

You'll find nifty deals on marked-down software at the computer or office supplies warehouse, and to make the deal even sweeter, the box often comes with a big round sticker that promises a manufacturer's rebate, too!

April. Tune into sales on TVs and VCRs. Spring fever has most consumers more interested in outdoor purchases than couch potato ones, so retailers are willing to deal. And with winter over, now's the time to schuss into that set of skis you coveted all winter—along with other cold-weather merchandise like snowmobiles, snow blowers, and space heaters. And don't forget after-Easter sales on decorations and candy. The trimmings will keep until next year and the sweets will be just as sweet next month.

May. Think Mother's Day and June brides and walk down the aisles with get-in the-mood sales on small appliances, silver, and fine china—the sorts of gifts retailers envision for the lady of the house. Then get in the swim with early-season sales on swimwear.

June. Summer gets into full swing, and as refrigerator doors across the country swing open over and over for cold drinks, compressors—the most expensive part of the machine—malfunction. So look for sales on iceboxes now, as well as Father's Day sales on Dad-oriented merchandise like tools and ties.

X Marks The Spot

If you live in or not far from a beach community, wait until September or October to shop for swimsuits and other summer clothing. Stores that stock—and mark way up—everything for the tourist know their market dries up once school starts, so they routinely reduce things 50 to 75 percent.

 The Bargain Hunter's [& Smart Consumer's] **Field Guide**

 Since the average shopper isn't thinking winter wear this month, it's a terrific time to snuggle up to great buys on fur coats. Conversely, it's also a great time to shop for swim wear as the retailer's summer season winds down and stores get nervous about how many bikinis they'll have left over and still in stock.

August. Go to the head of the class with pre-season sales on school supplies and end-of-season sales on watersports merchandise like surfboards, water skis, and scuba gear.

X Marks The Spot

If you're traveling and come upon an outlet mall (or if you happen to live near one), check out the bevy of name-brand designers' and manufacturers' shops. You can often find discounts on top of the already discounted prices. And don't forget to ask about unmarked specials!

September. Fall into deals on trees and shrubs as nurseries and garden departments prep for winter and clear out the last of summer's greenery. It's more fun to plant in autumn when the air is mild than in the heat of July, and the fruits of your labors get the whole of dormant winter to get settled before blooming again in spring. September's a terrific time to deal on not only plants but anything lawn and garden—patio furniture, barbecue grills, and mowers—because retailers want to clear out their stock for winter. And don't forget summer coolers like air conditioners and ceiling fans that aren't in hot demand any more.

October. Write your own toy story with pre-holiday sales on kids' stuff. This is another season for silver and fine china deals as stores seek to unload the last of the summer wedding stash. Fall is also—along with spring—new computer model season, so get dealing on those just-replaced units.

Treasure Chest Trivia

Retailers call the day after Thanksgiving, the day that starts their all-out blitz of holiday sales, Black Friday.

December. Make a list and check it twice with deals on office supplies, which are not on most shoppers' lists this month. Just before and after Christmas, shop till you drop for next season's (or even this year's) trimmings.

Start shopping for Christmas decorations—as well as lots of other merchandise—around the 18th of December. Stores often begin marking down holiday goods around then because—with less than a week to go until Santa puts in his appearance—they get antsy. They're worried that if their shelves aren't bare yet, they're not going to be.

But if you can, wait—it gets better. By December 26th, everything's down to 50 percent of what it was a couple of weeks earlier. And if you wait another week, prices can drop to 75 percent off.

This has an added bonus: Chanukah, Christmas, and Kwanzaa usually fall in different weeks of December. Which means that you can get terrific discounts on wares marked down after Christmas to give as gifts for the other holidays.

Treasure Chest Trivia

According to the National Retail Federation, stores make about 25 percent of their total year's sales during the winter holidays. No wonder they stock so much stuff!

On-Sale Star

Christmas isn't the only holiday on the retailer's calendar. Stores hold sales for patriotic events like President's Day, Memorial Day, and the Fourth of July, Valentine's Day, Easter, and Halloween, Labor Day and Thanksgiving, Father's Day, Mother's Day, and everything else they can come up with in between.

You can't think of anything? How about Super Bowl Savings, Back-to-School Values, or Swing-into-Spring sales? Sound familiar?

So even though some merchandise, like clothing, gets marked up as much as 100 percent, it also gets marked back down at least once a month. If you see something you like, be patient. Its turn as an on-sale star will come soon enough.

Chapter Three
The Three Bs: Buddy, Bulk, & Barter

Okay, you now know the 12 Secrets Of The Bargain Seeker. You know how to sniff out deals that may not even exist until you ask for them. But there's much more to savvy bargain hunting—you can also negotiate terrific deals when you use the three Bs: Buddy Buying, Bulk Buying, and Bartering. With the first two, you wield extra bargaining power through volume purchasing. And with bartering, you don't pay anything at all. In this chapter, we'll explore all three strategies.

The Buddy System

When you're a kid at summer camp, using the buddy system means you take a friend along on hikes so you can help each other out in the event of potential trailside dangers. When you're a bargain hunter, the buddy system still means you take a friend or colleague—or several friends or colleagues—along. But in this case, the reason is to help each other to greater savings.

As you already know, you can often get better deals if you buy multiples of an item. But there are some things you just don't need several of—unless you can go in with friends or family.

Making The Grade

Let's say, for example, that you're in the market for a cellular phone. The cell phone industry is becoming more competitive by the day, so the service you choose will be eager to make a deal so it can sign you up.

First, however, do your homework and comparison shop. Find out the following:

1. **Rates and rate plans.** What do various providers in your area charge? Do they have different plans for different needs? (Do they, for example, offer a special rate for those who don't plan to use the phone except for roadside emergencies as well as one for those who will use it a lot?)

2. **Coverage**. Some providers offer free calling nationwide; others charge for calls outside your geographic region. Some have a limited range in which their phones will work.

3. **Clarity and connectivity.** Some companies provide notoriously poor reception—calls don't go through or get cut off halfway through a conversation, while others in the same town are crystal clear.

4. **Customer service.** Some cell phone providers are terrific at handling billing problems and replacing lost or damaged phones; others need remedial customer service training.

You can easily get the answers to these questions. Look at the ads in your local newspaper. Stop in at providers' storefronts and ask. (Many have kiosks set up where you already shop, like at the mall, Wal-Mart, and Sam's Club.) You can also ask to use a phone for a few days to check reception for yourself. Ask friends and colleagues for reviews of the phone services they're signed with. Then choose the company that gets the best grades in all these areas.

Party Of Five

Now comes the buddy part. Ask your friends and family if they'd like to go in with you on new cellular phones. Since most people don't research before they buy, you'll find that several—long since frustrated with their current service—will readily agree.

Let's say three friends want to join you, and one wants a phone each for himself and his wife. So counting you, that's five phones. Which is real bargaining power.

Head to your chosen cellular provider and get ready to deal. When the salesperson approaches, say something like this:

You: *I'm interested in signing up for your service.*

Salesperson: *Good! We're offering a great deal; 20 cents a minute and no roaming. You can call across the country for free.*

You: *It's not going to be just me. I've got three associates who want to go in with me.*

Salesperson: *Good! All they have to do is sign our 20 cents a minute contract.*

You: *Altogether we'll be needing five phones. Can you work with us on your per-minute price?*

Salesperson: *Our price is already very competitive.*

You: *Yes, but that's for a single user. We're talking five here.*

Salesperson: *I could lower it to 15 cents a minute.*

You: *We'll be using the phones a lot. I'm not sure my people will go for that rate.*

Salesperson: *I'll have to check with my manager, but I could probably get it down to 12 cents for you.*

(She goes away, leaving you to examine the latest micro-mini phone, then comes back.)

Salesperson: *Okay, my manager says that for a party of five, we can certainly give you all the 12-cent rate.*

You: *Great. Now, what about this micro-mini phone? Is it new on the market?*

(You engage her in conversation about the phone.)

You: *What kind of deal can you give me on this phone?*

Salesperson: *Oh, I can't come down on its price at all. We just got it in last week.*

You: *I just brought in five new sales. Can you ask your manager?*

Salesperson: *He'll say no, but I'll ask.*

(She goes away again; then returns, all smiles)

Salesperson: *He'll give you the phone for 20 percent off.*

You: *Thank you!*

Expedition Tip

Cell phone providers sometimes offer free earlier-model phones when you sign up. But just because you get the phone doesn't mean you get off scot-free. You may still want extra batteries and a quick charger and a case, which can add up to $100 or more. Be sure to negotiate a discount on these items before you leave the store.

Eating For Two—Or Ten

What do you do when you come across a deal like 47 jars of fancy preserves imported from France, ten cases of gourmet cocoa, or 50 gift boxes of fine Italian pasta and olive oil—all for a fraction of the retail cost if you buy them all?

Call your friends and invite them to participate. By the time you divvy up the goods, you've all got gourmet goodies galore plus enough to give as great hostess or holiday gifts.

If you're an expatriate of another country or even another state, you know how you crave that certain something you just can't get in your new digs. Cans of Philips Crab Soup from Maryland or special sausage from Germany—ya gotta have it.

In Rob's family, where they know great Mexican food, whoever makes the three-hour drive to Tijuana buys enough tortillas and *pan dulce* (sweet breads) to divvy among several households—or almost enough. They're inexpensive when bought in-country, and they're *delicioso*.

We once brought back 12 dozen flour and five dozen corn tortillas from Guerrero Negro, a small town in the Baja peninsula. In two weeks there wasn't a single one left.

In South Florida, Art's area, everybody who goes home to New York for a visit brings cartons of matzohs back south. It's not that you can't buy them in South Florida; it's that they're cheaper in the Big Apple.

BUSINESS BEACON
Dirty Laundry

You know there's strength in numbers. When you're talking about purchases, that strength translates into volume buying.

If you have a small business, however, this often presents a problem. You can only use—and have room to store—so many industrial-sized rolls of plastic wrap, boxes of packing peanuts, or widgets at a time. So you find yourself unable to take advantage of volume discounts.

Unless you buy the bargain hunter's way, which is to band together with others in your industry to buy in volume.

Say you've got a cozy bed-and-breakfast inn and you find a wholesale supplier that will sell you 50 dozen luxury cotton sheets for 25 percent off what you'd pay if you bought retail, plus an additional 15 percent if you buy in volume.

continued on page 41

You can do the same: Put together an informal buyers club of family and friends from the same region. Then, whenever somebody travels home, they can bring back enough for the crowd.

That's Bulk

Like buddy buying, bulk buying works because you can negotiate terrific discounts when you purchase in volume. But where you use the buddy system to purchase more products or services than you or your company alone can use, you employ bulk buying when you can indeed utilize all of a product. The secret is to be creative with how you use those goods as well as how you bargain for them.

How would you like, for instance, to redecorate the floors of your home, office, or shop with exquisite imported ceramic tile for less than the cost of serviceable old vinyl or lineoleum? Install new designer carpet in any room for the price of a throw rug? Sound impossible? It's not if you're a savvy bargain hunter.

But with only six guest rooms, you'd never use 600 sheets unless you didn't do laundry for months on end. And who'd want to be stuck in a laundry room with 600 dirty bed linens?

Not you—and you don't have to be! Call or e-mail the other lodging providers in your area and ask them to buy with you. (Yes, they're your competitors, but they should also be part of your network of associates.) When 10 of you go in together, you each get five dozen—a workable amount—and you each also get the 15 percent volume discount.

You'll accomplish these miracles with end lots. These are the home improvement retailer's version of refrigerator leftovers and you'll find them in carpet and tile outlets, wall covering centers and of course, home improvement superstores like Lowe's and Home Depot. Instead of too much meatloaf or a Tupperware container full of mashed potatoes, these stores get stuck with too much carpet, tile, linoleum, or wallpaper.

This is frequently because of a miscalculation from somebody else's project. The contractor or the customer special-orders a particular product and discovers at the end of the job that they didn't need anywhere near that much. So instead of paying for it, they leave it for the store to dispose of. Sometimes customers will order an entire project's worth of tile or carpet and then never bother to pay for it and pick it up.

For the bargain hunter, both of these situations are like finding money. If you're willing to be flexible with your own home improvement ideas, you can redecorate virtually for pennies with elegant designer materials you might never otherwise dream of affording.

Gem Hunting

How do you find these gems? Take a spin through the store. You'll usually find ceramic tile overruns or unclaimed special orders stacked on pallets near the back of the shop. Look for these first—the stuff that's glued up on display boards near the front of the store is good for getting ideas about what's new, what's hot, and what going prices are, but it's geared toward the average consumer, not the wily bargain seeker. Occasionally end lots and overruns will be tagged with a discounted price, but often they're not marked at all. When you find a pallet or stack of tiles that looks promising, approach the manager and inquire about the price.

* *This tile looks interesting. What's it going for?*   **OR**
* *I see you've got this tile marked at **X** percent off. Could you do any better if I bought the whole pallet?*

If she doesn't seem too amenable, help her decide. Remind her that if you don't buy the whole thing she might sell a few boxes here and there and then end up with only a couple left—not enough for anybody to be able to use, and so not enough to ultimately sell.

* *If I take the whole thing right now it's out of your hair. You don't have to worry about getting stuck with any of it later.*

Expedition Tip

Team up with your neighbors to negotiate deals on services like yard maintenance, pest control, and even home alarm systems. When you offer providers several homes in a single block or neighborhood, they're impressed—and ready to bargain. You also get the advantage of power in numbers; providers will give a better level of service to keep everyone's business than they might to keep one person's.

   The Bargain Hunter's [& Smart Consumer's] **Field Guide**

Remember that this is a friendly exchange. You want the manager to realize you're serious about your offer, but you definitely don't want to be belligerent or demeaning. Some would-be bargainers get into trouble by issuing a challenge. Their entire body language says, "Look, buddy-roo, either you sell it to me or you don't sell it to nobody. Take your pick." This is not the true bargain hunter's style.

If the manager doesn't accept your offer, that's her choice. She knows more about her store and the management style of those above her (which she has to satisfy) than you do. So make it a game. If she can play along you'll both have a ball. If not, you needn't buy at the set price. That's your choice.

Serendipity

Half the fun of this sort of bargain hunting is its sense of serendipity. You may go into the store looking for beige linoleum and come home with pink marble, terra-cotta tile, or honey oak parquet. Naturally, you don't want to buy something that won't match your décor no matter how you look at it, or something you just don't like, but use your imagination. It may not be what you had in mind to begin with, but if you can make it work, why not?

BUSINESS BEACON
Build Out

Save money when you lease retail or office space. Instead of paying the lessor to build out your quarters, do it yourself with bargained-for materials and construction services.

Sometimes the price is so incredible that you can be a big spender (for relative pennies) and give somebody else a wonderful surprise. When Rob's parents bought a new apartment, we sent them boxes of $4 per-square-foot oak parquet that we'd picked up for 25 cents a square foot to redo their floors.

X Marks The Spot

Shipping heavy items cross-country can be prohibitively expensive—unless you buy them an airline ticket. We sent about 150 pounds of parquet from Florida to California for only $70 by sending it air cargo via Delta Airlines. The same overnight service through FedEx or UPS would have cost over $300.

Magic Carpet

Because carpet comes on huge rolls, anywhere from 90 to 180 yards, carpet dealers almost always have remnants. When customers buy a certain number of yards there's always something left over. And as with ceramic tile, you can also sometimes find expensive designer carpet that's been special-ordered and then never claimed. Also as with ceramic tile, these carpet dealer's woes can lead to terrific deals for the bargain hunter.

How to do you know what to look for? As with tile, don't go to the samples glued up on boards at the front of the showroom. Those are for the consumer who wants to pay full price. Instead, nose around the back of the store. You'll see rolls of varying thicknesses, colors and styles propped against the walls or laid out on the floor. These are the ones you're interested in.

Make friends with the manager or owner. Tell him what you're looking for. Ask a few questions about the remnants. Most people love to talk about their work and like nothing better than for somebody else to show a healthy interest in their world. This is how you develop a rapport—and a sales buddy you can go back to again and again.

While you're making conversation, and a sales ally, ask these kinds of questions:

* *Is this a popular style?*
* *Do many people go for this unusual color?*
* *I see shag carpet is in again. Are you selling much of it?*

Seeing The Light

End lots don't have to be all about floor coverings. You may walk into the store intending to buy light bulbs and come across an entire tray of flashlights marked at 50 percent off or more. That's what happened to us a couple weeks before Christmas. We picked up all of them and tucked them in with the shirts (75 percent off at an outlet center) we'd bought for the guys on our list. They were a big hit.

After all, what male can resist a flashlight—or any other hardware store gizmo? When we found a bin of marked-down tool sets—pliers and screwdrivers in pre-packaged kits—we scooped them up, too. They made great last-minute gifts for unexpected guests.

 The Bargain Hunter's [& Smart Consumer's] Field Guide

* *What would you recommend for a living room that's going to get a lot of wear and tear? (Or a guest bedroom that won't be used very often or whatever you're looking for?)*

  If your new buddy points you to a carpet that's way beyond what you're willing to spend, say so.
* *That's out of my price range. How about this one over here?*

  If that one's high as well, be honest.
* *That's more than what I wanted to spend. What else do you have?*

It's okay to let him know you're sniffing out a deal. You're not being cheap—you're buying smart. And instead of working against him, you're enlisting his help. So now's the time when he'll show you the real deals, the pieces he probably wouldn't bring to the average shopper's attention.

Expedition Tip

Retailers often reward their sales associates with a spiff—a monetary bonus—for selling package deals. Which means that salesman *wants* to work with you. If he can negotiate a sale where you buy not just the computer but the printer, scanner and extended warranty contract as well, for instance, he's in heaven. So by bargaining your way to a great deal, you're helping him put extra money in his pocket, too!

Expedition Tip

Always, *always* remember to thank the vendor or manager for giving you the deal. People like to be appreciated no matter what the situation is, and especially when they're essentially—by giving you a deal—also giving you money.

Ceramic and vinyl tile often gets marked down because the style has been discontinued. If you or your installer makes a major goof on installation- or if you gouge a hole in it next year, there's no going back for another box. Keep this in mind and consider buying an extra box.

Don't Be Square

End lots aren't just for carpet and vinyl. You'll find the same terrific deals on linoleum and vinyl tile, and for all the same reasons.

What do you look for? Once again, don't go to those glued-on sample squares first. For linoleum, seek out odd-sized rolls propped in corners or in special bargain bins.

For vinyl tile, find the boxes stacked on pallets at the back of the store or stuck out in the aisles. Then head for the manager and start negotiating.

When you buy odd boxes of ceramic or vinyl tile make sure each one has the same *run number,* which you'll find stamped on the box. They may all look the same and have the same name, but there can be significant variations in colors or shading. If you're not careful, you can end up with a floor that looks like a muddle of end lots.

What happens if that's all there is left? Three boxes of tile with three different run numbers won't look very good—unless you get creative. If you've got small rooms like bathrooms, foyers or laundry rooms, you can use

BARGAIN HUNTER'S JOURNAL
Carpet Ride

We carpeted our entire house in a top-of-the-line Berber for $175. We weren't looking for Berber—in fact we'd always claimed we weren't too crazy about it. But when we came upon 166 yards of the stuff originally priced at $1,900 and negotiated it down to $175, we couldn't resist.

Why was it such a steal? One reason was that somebody had apparently dragged it across an entire warehouse or possibly even an oil-slicked driveway, and the once-light oatmeal color was dirty and torn. Nobody in their right mind would want to buy it. Except us. (We looked beneath the top layer of drudge and found that the rest of the roll was perfect.)

Another reason was that the roll—which had been special-ordered and

continued on page 47

one box for each room and nobody but (possibly) you will notice the difference. Or get creative when you lay out your floor. You can plan a "natural variation" in shades, a checkerboard or herringbone effect—or go even more eclectic.

Several years ago we purchased several hundred pounds of gorgeous pink-veined marble in Tijuana, Mexico, carted it 2,500 miles across the country to a beach condo we'd bought in South Carolina, and installed it six feet high behind the tub and along the walls— only to discover we didn't quite have enough to cover the floor. Solution: we laid the rest of our tile in a border around the room and placed carpet that matched the bedroom in the center. And it worked! It looked classy and was actually warmer under cold-morning feet than marble would have been.

Odd Lots

The retailer will frequently give you an even better bargain if you take more than one end lot off his hands and make a package deal. You have to be willing then never claimed—was 15 feet wide, and the display/cutting machine at the store can only handle 12 feet rolls. So this poor bedraggled roll had been in the back room for nearly a year and had never seen even the fluorescent light of day.

As a final reason for the department manager to discount it to us, we showed up right before inventory, the time all retailers dread because they have to account to the corporate office for every unsold item.

By the way, we decided we love Berber. It's in, it's classy, and it feels good beneath bare feet.

to move quickly—before another bargain hunter comes along—and you have to think fast about *where* you can use those sometimes odd-sized lots, but you can come away with terrific deals.

Instead of buying only that perfect shade of rose for the bathroom floor, offer to take those boxes of Mexican pavers for the kitchen, and how about that stack of pickled oak parquet for the entry hall? By going the package deal route, you can redecorate three rooms of your home for less than the price of doing one at retail. If you hadn't planned on redoing every room in the house quite yet, but the deal's too good to pass up (and doesn't pinch your pocketbook), go for it anyway. You can store the extra materials in the garage until you've got time to do it yourself or until you negotiate a great deal with an installer. (More on this in Chapter 6.)

Like end lots, package deals aren't just for flooring. The entire shopping world is full of possibilities. We discovered the joys of books on tape during our travels across country—and we also discovered an audio books vendor at a swap meet in Southern California who carries just about every title you can imagine. Every year we visit this fellow, make our selections of tapes that in the retail store would sell for $14.95 and up, and then make a deal. Like this:

Us: *Wow, you've got some great stuff here. These unabridged Stephen King stories should take us at least through west Texas. How much do you want for them?.*
Vendor: *They're $10 each.*
Us: *We've chosen five really good ones. Could you do a little better?*
Vendor: *Nope, they cost me almost that much wholesale.*
Us: *What if we got these three Patricia Cornwells and two Star Treks, too?*
Vendor: *Ten tapes. Hmmm…I could give them to you for $6 apiece.*
Us: *Thank you!*

BUSINESS BEACON
Filtering Profits

Don Hogan of Panama City Beach, Florida used to own a chain of tune-up shops and was always in the market for oil and air filters. Don discovered that often a filter manufacturer will decide to take over a particular market, such as all the discount or automotive centers in a region. So they'll buy out the stores' entire existing stock of their competitors' filters and put theirs in place instead.

What to do with all those oil and air filters? They don't want them back on the market for consumers to buy. Don decided to make them a deal they couldn't refuse. He offered to buy each and every filter for 25 cents apiece and was gladly sold three tractor-trailer loads. Which he resold to customers at his tune-up shops for $5 each. That's business bargain hunting!

Barter Jargon

While most people never, ever consider it (or have even heard of it in more than a passing sense), bartering is one the best bargain-hunting strategies on the planet. When you barter, you get goods and services for free. What could be better?

You don't, of course, get something for nothing. You have to provide goods or services in exchange for the ones you "buy." And while you can't pop into your local Wal-Mart, for instance, and barter for the products on the shelves, there are lots of places to effectively barter for all sorts of things. We know of one prominent national publishing company that uses bartering exclusively—they don't purchase anything outright.

So how exactly do you go about bartering? First, get creative and think about what you can offer. If you're an entrepreneur, this may be a snap. Services—from bookkeeping to catering to car repair to landscape maintenance to web site design and much, much more—are always in demand. So is merchandise of all kinds.

If you're not a business owner, you probably have skills, hobbies, and just plain time to offer. You can trade homebaked cookies, your green thumb with garden maintenance or design, your expertise as a handyman or woman, your skill with a sewing machine or knitting needles, or—always in demand—your time and nurturing attention as a babysitter.

BUSINESS BEACON
Retail For (Whole)Sale

Yes, you're a business owner. But that doesn't mean you have to buy all your merchandise from wholesalers. Just by keeping your eyes open and your bargain antennae tuned, you can pick up great deals from regular retailers.

If you're a plumber, for instance, you can often find kitchen or bathroom faucets that normally retail for $45 going for $6 to $20 at home improvement warehouses or discount stores like Kmart. When you do, buy them all.

Even if you have to keep them in inventory for a while, it's worth it. It saves you money, and if you want to be a good guy or gal you can pass the savings on to your customers, who'll remember. They'll not only call on you again the next time, but also refer you to friends.

continued on page 50

Next, consider who you'll barter with. If you're handy with a hammer, for instance, or you have a construction or cabinet-making company, you might barter with your dentist: cleaning and x-rays in exchange for building a set of bookcases in his office. Trade a summer's harvest of fresh vegetables from your garden for a set of summer togs for your toddler at a local baby boutique. Teach a local restaurateur to speak French in exchange for meals. The possibilities are limitless!

What happens if you find a particular product on sale at a perfect price and you're set to buy out the store—but they only have two left in stock? Ask for a rain check. Some stores have a set policy in which they'll guarantee the sale price as soon as they get that item restocked, or they'll specially order it for you.

If you've got a home furnishings shop, you can pick up assemble-it-yourself furniture for 50 to 75 percent off when the manufacturer discontinues the line. All you have to do is cobble it together and sell it as is, or get creative and paint or stencil it.

Remember that part of your bargaining power is in buying all the store has in stock. When you offer to take everything, it makes an impression. The store is there to sell, and when they make a major sale to you, they're as happy as you are.

BUSINESS BEACON

Exchange City

Business-to-business bartering is smart business. Trade your accounting services for advertising production and placement from a local ad agency. Exchange off-season or weeknight lodging at your bed & breakfast for linens from a supplier. Offer your company's wholesale polo shirts screenprinted with custom logos for a computer manufacturer's products.

continued on page 51

50   The Bargain Hunter's [& Smart Consumer's] Field Guide

Work one-on-one with local businesses or companies across the country (or even the world) by contacting them directly. Or join a barter exchange that acts as a marketplace for members to advertise their wares and services, and then facilitates trades indirectly among members. At Intagio (www.intagio.com), for example, you get a Web page in which to showcase your stuff. When another business buys from you, the trade "dollars" are placed in your account, which you can then use to purchase goods, services, or even a vacation from any other member.

Keep in mind that the IRS considers trade dollars to be the same as hard cash—you're expected to charge and pay tax on bartered items, and to report them to Uncle Sam. As well, barter exchanges may charge membership and service fees.

Find barter exchanges by going to your favorite search engine (www.google.com is great) and typing in "barter exchange."

Expedition Tip

Band together with a group of friends to form a babysitters' circle. Members barter time—for each hour or evening of child care you put in, you get equal child care time from another member.

Chapter Four
Secondhand Rose

Some people love anything old, whether it's a 400 year-old antique or a four year-old cast-off. For some, it's the history that hooks them, the fact that a particular piece might have rubbed elbows with (or been rubbed by the elbows of) a Civil War belle, a turn-of-the-last-century beau, or a Victorian duchess or parlor maid. For others, the magic is in the character of a piece—especially something that's well-worn and obviously been beloved—and the mystery of who once owned it and what their lives were like. For still others, it's the excitement of finding something still functional and fashionable, and gloriously inexpensive because it's secondhand. (And sometimes worth a small fortune, as buyers discover on TV programs like PBS' popular *Antiques Road Show.)*

All this stuff is not only a bargain hunter's playground, but one of the hottest trends going. Barbra Streisand may have bemoaned secondhand goods in the song "Secondhand Rose," but recycled merchandise is in these days. Turn to any decorating book, magazine, or TV show and you'll see room after room decked out in old furniture, fabrics, and accessories. Entire stores are devoted to second hand clothing, toys, tools, and furnishings. And these aren't dreary Salvation Army way stations, but bright, cheerful, trendy boutiques where you're as likely to see Mercedes and BMWs in the parking lot as rusty Pontiacs.

Why the sudden popularity? First, it's fun. The Baby Boomers who started their young-adult lives combing thrift shops for outlandish clothing with which to horrify their parents have come full circle (except now *we're* the parents) and decided that everything old really is new again. And second, we've ricocheted away from the old Eighties mentality of "more is better" conspicuous spending to a new focus on home and family. Cocooning is in. People want to be surrounded by things that feel comfortably warm and cozy—and what better way to achieve that sensuous sensation than with things that have been around a long time?

Previously-loved merchandise comes in many forms, from antiques with the elegant patina of age to garage sale cast-offs awaiting a new lease on life. In this chapter we explore how to sift the silver chalice from the tin cup and how to bargain with both the amateur salesperson and the professional auctioneer.

Treasure Chest Trivia

What's the difference between an antique and a collectible? It depends on who you ask, but generally speaking an antique is anything more than 50 years old. (Some experts will tell you 75 years or 100 years, so you be the judge.) A collectible, then, is anything younger than 50 or so—including, perhaps, some Baby Boomers.

That's Garage, Not Garbage

Thanks to the old adage "one man's trash is another man's treasure," garage, yard, and tag sales can be fertile ground for the bargain hunter. What's the difference? There really isn't one, except for the minor differences of whether it's held in a garage (and on the driveway) or spread across a yard. And despite the fact that either of these can be called a tag sale, in many cases nothing's tagged at all. You have to ask. (Which is terrific, because the act of asking paves the way for bargaining.)

Whatever they choose to call them, people hold these sales for a variety of reasons and have various expectations of their financial outcome. Just as you do when you shop retail stores, you'll need to understand where the seller is coming from in order to negotiate the best deal. Here's a rundown of the types of sales and the best bargaining techniques for each.

(Some sales, like moving and multi-family sales, usually advertise themselves as such, either in ads in the newspaper or shopper, or on handmade signs leading to them—but you won't always know before you go.)

* **The moving sale.** This one's an all-star. Once people start packing for a move, they realize just how much *stuff* they've accumulated. And then they realize that they really don't want to pack it all up and cart it to their new digs. They also often decide that their furniture won't fit in their new home for reasons of space or aesthetics. Or they decide (consciously or not) to start over fresh. Whatever the reason, they don't want to haul everything across town or across country. Solution: garage sale. You'll find all sorts of high-quality stuff at terrific prices at a moving sale. And since the seller's more motivated than most to get rid of his possessions, he's very open to haggling. Bargain hunting rating: ★★★★★

* **Multi-family.** This type of sale, in which a group of neighbors pitch in to share the work and fun of setting up and staffing, has been planned in advance. Which means everybody's had time to consider what they're going to sell and dig it out of the attic, unearth it from the depths of Junior's closet, or pry it from Dad's hands. Nobody wants to be the one with the least to contribute, so they all bring as much as they can. And nobody wants their neighbors to see their collection of microwave-abused Tupperware, so they leave the really yucky stuff for the trash man. Thus, there's plenty to choose from and the quality is keen. As another multi-family bonus, everybody's in a party mood, so they're ready to haggle and have fun. Bargain hunting rating: ★★★★★

* **Mini-estate sale.** This is the one that's staged when Gramps or Gramma passes away or goes to the nursing home, leaving behind belongings that no one in the family wants. Some people call in estate specialists to handle the sale, but others just cart everything out to the garage or yard and host it themselves. You'll come across great finds like antique furniture and dishes and vintage clothing, but be prepared for depressing products, too—bed pans, potty chairs, and other accoutrements of invalid life, as well as stretched-out sweaters and misshapen shoes that make you wonder if that's what a person's life comes down to. Bargain hunting rating: ★★★

* **Cleaned house or garage.** Could be nifty—or not. Sometimes people get in a spring-cleaning frenzy and decide to
sell everything. At others, the garage sale is (for you
anyway) an unsatisfactory alternative to the dump. Definitely check this one out but don't put it at the top of your
list. Bargain hunting rating: ★★
* **Sounds like fun.** Here we have the kissing cousin to the
cleaned-house variety. It's usually not very good because
it's too spur of the moment and the seller doesn't really
have anything to sell. Worth a drive-by but usually no
more. Bargain hunting rating: ★
* **Needs the money.** This is about on a par with the spring
cleaning sale. You might walk away with something
wonderful. And you might just as easily come away with
nothing. Bargain hunting rating: ★★
* **The professional.** You'll recognize this one because they're
usually out there every weekend or so and their attitudes
are more professional than the casual householder's. The
deals you get won't be as good because the professional's
learned to haggle, too, but you'll still do far better than if
you went regular retail. Bargain hunting rating: ★★★

X Marks The Spot

Make buddies with that professional garage saler. If you're looking
for something in particular that he doesn't have, put him on the alert
and have him hunt it down for you. He gets a mission—and a
potentially guaranteed sale—and you get that whatsit you've been
seeking.

The Serendipity Guide

How do you find garage sales? It's easy. One way is simply to let
serendipity be your guide. Hop in the car on any sunny weekend
morning and start cruising likely neighborhoods. You'll soon spot
hand-lettered signs beckoning you to all sorts of enticing finds.

Sales in middle-income neighborhoods are usually the best because people have enough money to have bought all sorts of stuff and be able to dispose of it without a qualm. Lower income areas won't yield much because residents don't have much to part with, and really ritzy areas aren't so hot because people who have pots of money are wary of strangers roaming around their turf. You'll also often find great yard sales on country lanes—country people tend to be terrific collectors, and when they decide to clean house, they rely on a stream of out-for-a-Sunday-drivers to provide their clientele.

Another way is to check out the *garage sales* section in your local newspaper or shopper (you know, those Thrifty Nickel/Pennysaver throwaway publications that are all ads.) It might seem silly to check the paper when you can find lots of sales simply by cruising, but these ads can alert you to sales in unfamiliar neighborhoods you might not have known about. They usually contain descriptions of the type of wares that will be on view, and can even help you plan your route. (Our daily paper thoughtfully keys ads by neighborhood and provides a take-along map.)

Up With The Sun

What's the best time to hit garage and yard sales? It depends on your goals—and your early-rising capabilities. In some areas, garage sales start early. Very early. Like 7 a.m. Which means the really rabid shoppers, including dealers scouting merchandise for antiques stores and flea markets, often show up even earlier. So if you want to get the best pick of all the goods on offer, you've got to grab that coffee go-cup and be out the door while the sun's still on the rise.

On the other hand, sellers aren't particularly motivated to bargain while the dew's still on the grass. They've got a whole day ahead of them in which to sell their stuff. But since most people start garage-sale hunting early, the day starts winding down sometime after three in the afternoon. Customers dwindle. Sellers who have been up and at 'em since dawn get tired—and anxious to get rid of whatever's left. The prospect of dragging unsold wares back inside and putting things away (especially when they thought they'd seen the last of it) is not appealing. So when you show up at the last minute, that garage sale merchant is delighted to see you. And in the mood to bargain.

The obvious problem with this technique is that if you wait until the 11th hour, you run the risk of there being nothing left worth buying. What's a bargain hunter to do? Play it both ways. Start shopping early. If you see something you like but you think it's a bit

pricey, ask the seller to come down. If you can't negotiate the price
you want—and you're willing to run the risk of it being snatched up
by someone else—go on your merry way. You can always come back
late in the day when the seller will be more motivated.

Here's what you say at eight in the morning:

> **You:** How much do you want for this dresser?
> **Seller:** A hundred and fifty.
> **You:** Gee, that's more than I can spend. Would you take a
> hundred?
> **Seller** (watching several other cars full of eager potential
> buyers pull up): No, we're pretty firm on one-fifty.
> **You:** What if I took the bed, too?
> **Seller** (watching people swarming toward the bed and
> dresser): I'm afraid not.
> **You:** OK. Maybe I'll stop back later and see if you've still
> got them.
> **Seller:** Sure. We'll be here.

And you toddle off to the next sale. You make it a point to return
at four in the afternoon, the dead zone of the garage sale day. And to
your delight, the dresser and bed are still sitting out on the driveway,
along with the seller, who perks up slightly at your arrival. You
approach the fellow.

> **You:** Hi. How'd the day go? It looks like you sold a lot.
> **Seller** (who's kicked back, exhausted, in a lawn chair): Yeah,
> we did pretty good.
> **You:** I'm still interested in the dresser. Could you do a little
> better than one-fifty?
> **Seller:** I don't know, I'd have to ask my wife (calls her over
> from the garage where she's trying to figure out what to do
> with the things that didn't sell). Honey, what could we take
> for that old dresser?
> **Wife:** Well, we had it marked at a hundred and fifty.
> **You:** I could give you $90 if you threw in the matching bed.
> **Wife** (looking at empty street): That was an expensive set
> when we bought it.
> **You:** It's a nice set. But I'm buying it for my son's room and
> you know how kids are on furniture…

Wife (looking back at unsold wares on driveway): Well, I
  suppose we could take $100 for it.
Seller: We've got an old quilt that goes with it, too. We had
  it marked at $40, but we'd give you all three pieces for $125.
You: Great. Thank you!

Garage Sale Finds

What kinds of things can you expect to find at garage sales? You
never know for certain, and that's what makes them fun. Since garage
sale sellers are more unsophisticated in terms of what they've got
than an antiques shop or flea market entrepreneur, you can find
terrific collectibles like art pottery, Depression glass, toys, and
vintage lunch boxes (yes, they're very collectible!) for pennies.

Garage and yard sales are also great places to pick up vintage
clothing (very trendy), linens like quilts, comforter sets, and towels,
and items like books and furniture. You'll find tools, sewing, knitting, and crafts materials (all those enthusiastically begun hobbies
that fizzled), dishes, pictures, kitchen gizmos, costume jewelry, baby
items like walkers and strollers, and Christmas ornaments.

You'll also find a lot of junk—old plastic margarine tubs, books
with titles like *Advanced Studies in Synthetic Chemical Modeling,*
ancient computers and printers, anemic plastic flowers, and sheets
that last looked fresh in 1957.

Expedition Tip

Take plenty of cash. Garage sale sellers will usually take a check, but
will be much happier—and thus much more willing to bargain—if
you give them good old greenbacks. It not only relieves them of the
fear that your check will bounce but also makes a satisfying display
when you pull out a wad of notes in mid-negotiation.

The Five Rules Of Thumb

Bargain hunting at garage sales can be a boon or a bust, depending
on a variety of factors. Follow these Five Rules of Thumb for finding
the best driveway deals.

1. **Season.** Spring and summer are ideal yard sale seasons. The
    weather's balmy, the sun rises early, and people enjoy sitting

outdoors interacting with passersby. But there's more to it than weather. By summer, people have come to the realization that all those gadgets they got for Christmas—the handy hotdog/bun/corn-on-the-cob steamer, show-every-pore lighted cosmetic mirror, and routing/drilling/hammering tool—are never going to be used, and they're ready to get rid of them.

Which is great for the bargain hunter. If you can pick up a $30 doohickey yard-sale-priced at $10 for only $5, you can afford to take the chance that you'll never use it, either. And as a final summer bonus, it gets hot and sticky sitting in the sun all day. By three in the afternoon or so, people are more than willing to give you a great deal just so they can get rid of things, close down, and go inside out of the heat.

Although spring and summer are ideal, there is no bad yard sale season, so don't stop cruising when the weather turns cooler. You never, ever know when you'll find the deal of a lifetime!

2. **Neighborhood.** You'll find different goods in new neighborhoods filled with young families than in older ones where people have lived for years. If you're looking for baby things and toys, hit the new tracts. If it's vintage wares you want, try streets of old homes first.

3. **Seller's attachment.** Most people you meet at garage sales are genuinely friendly and a lot of fun. But some few curmudgeons are convinced that their well-worn cast-offs are worth an awful lot more than is reasonable, almost as if they don't actually want to sell anything. If you bump up against one of these—and you can tell right away by their attitude—don't argue. Here's a sample:

You: *How much are you asking for this old radio?*
Seller (coldly): *That's $65.*
You: *Could you take $50?*
Seller (still cold): *I wouldn't take a dime less than $65. That's what it's worth.*
You: *Have a nice day.*

Arguing isn't worth the effort; they won't change their minds. Smile and move on.

4. **Sophistication.** Some people either don't really know what they have or don't care. To them the whole point of the exercise is to enjoy the sun, meet nice folks, get rid of stuff,

and make a little money. Others—especially those few who hold garage sales as a part-time income opportunity—can tell cut crystal from pressed glass and are not about to let you buy the first for the price of the second. You can haggle with these people, but be aware that it's going to be a bigger challenge than with the householder on a weekend selling spree.

5. **Sense of humor.** Most garage sale sellers are more than willing to admit that those throw pillows have seen better days or that the bicycle is a bit rusty—that's why they're selling them cheap. But you can run into a select few people who can't take any criticism of their belongings. As a member of the bargain hunter's guild, you know not to insult a seller's wares and you won't do it. But those few humorless souls out there tend to take normal haggling as a blow to their pride. Again, smile and move on to the vast cheerful majority who are a delight to deal with.

White Elephants And Jumbles

Not all garage sales are found in garages. There's also the rummage sale, the white elephant sale, the jumble sale (a basically British term), the parking lot sale, and the storage space sale.

The rummage, white elephant, and jumble sales are all variations on a theme. As a fund-raiser for a church, PTA, or other nonprofit organization, everybody contributes some sort of tchochkes that are sold in the hall or auditorium. Actually, the names seem in danger of becoming antiques themselves—which is too bad because they're delightfully descriptive: you *rummage* through a *jumble* of other people's *white elephants,* belongings that are useless to their owners but too good to throw away.

The parking lot sale is one that businesses stage to get rid of old inventory or furniture. Where we live, for instance, in an area with lots of small beachfront motels, you'll often find an impromptu sale

[If you're looking for baby things and toys, hit the new tracts.]

of guest-worn dressers, headboards, bedspreads, and even beach-motif pictures. And while you probably wouldn't want any of it in your bedroom as-is, it's perfect for painting and decorating into something new, for furnishing a rental unit, or even for setting up Babs in her first college apartment.

And what about the storage space sale? People who've stashed their stuff in mini-warehouses sooner or later reach the point where they're sick of shuttling back and forth for belongings they once thought indispensable. So they hold a no-holds barred sale. Which is good for you and them!

> [Set up Babs in her first college apartment with re-newly chic furnishings from hotel parking lot sales.]

Expedition Tip

Not all garage sales take place on weekends. In some parts of the country, they're held on Fridays as well as Saturdays, and in some regions they even start on Thursdays.

Garage and yard sales aren't merely for the homeowner out for a weekend drive. As a business owner, you can find all sorts of stuff, from wares for resale to supplies for restocking, at garage and yard sales.

One entrepreneur we know, who runs a thriving electronics sales and repair company, shops garage sales for ailing TVs and computers. He fixes them and then sells them for a profit, or uses their parts to fix other units in his workshop. Another entrepreneur, a seamstress, haunts tag sales for old clothing she recycles into gorgeous garb for her customers. A talented artist hunts down glassware she decorates and sells.

Depending on your business, you might shop yard sales for collectibles for resale, or for funky furniture to repaint or refinish and market.

continued on page 64

The Bargain Hunter's Garage Sale/Flea Market Checklist:

Every good Scout knows the importance of being prepared. Make the most of your outdoor expeditions with this got-it?-good! list of things to bring.

- ❑ Comfortable shoes
- ❑ Layered clothing
- ❑ Hat and sunscreen
- ❑ Handy but tucked-away cash (no need to tempt pick-pockets)
- ❑ Notebook for jotting down addresses or space numbers of sellers you want to revisit
- ❑ If in the midst of a particular decorating project, paint chips, wallpaper/fabric samples, and window or room measurements (You never know when you'll luck onto a carpet remnant or potential window covering.)
- ❑ Tape measure
- ❑ Magnet for testing metals (If it doesn't stick, that object is brass, silver, bronze, or gold. If it does, you're looking at a cheaper base metal.)
- ❑ Cheat sheet with clothing sizes of near and dear ones
- ❑ Coffee or cold drink go-cup
- ❑ Wet wipes for cleaning up after digging through troves of dusty, rusty, grimy potential treasures
- ❑ Tote or shopping bag(s) for carrying away treasures

Garage Sale Gem Guidelines

When you discover those garage or yard sale gems that are electronic or mechanical marvels (or not), it's important to ask whether the thing works. There's no point in carting home a prize that you paid only pennies for if you discover when you get it home that it was sold cheap because it's a non-starter.

Tag sale sellers are usually wonderfully honest. If that toaster, TV set, or table saw malfunctions, they'll let you know. But in most cases you have to ask. Now, just as with buying damaged goods from the retail superstore, just because the thing's ailing doesn't mean it's not a good buy. In some cases, all you have to do is graft on a new plug. In others it might be a bad fuse that's easily replaced or a corroded battery contact that can be sanded down. And remember that if an item isn't in working order, you've got real bargaining power.

So how do you know what might be a good bet and what's something best left for the trash man? Follow these simple guidelines.

* Always ask to plug in electronic items and try them out.
* Keep in mind that TV sets can display a perfect picture for an hour or two and then go fuzzy. Obviously, you're not going to sit in someone's driveway and watch while the hours tick by, so if you've got doubts, use them as a negotiating tool.

Garage sales are also terrific places to shop for furnishings and accessories for your business. Look, for instance, for books for kids and adults with which to furnish your lobby or waiting room (or your bed-and-breakfast inn); for art prints and plates to dress up your office; or for vintage launderable linens to spill out of drawers and cupboards in your retail shop.

All it takes to turn garage sale finds into business bonuses are your bargain-hunting antennae and a little imagination.

[Shopping garage sales for your business is smart business.]

✳   If the product has accessories, make sure they're all present.
     If they're not, you've got a bargaining chip.

Calling All Fleas

In some parts of the country it's a flea market; in others it's a swap
meet. But whatever you call it, this eclectic conglomeration of goods
is a bargain seeker's Ultimate Mission, jam-packed with deals. It's
also one of the few places in America where sellers expect to dicker.
Many merchandisers have staked their claims through their own
knowledge of bargain hunting and spend their non-sales days track-
ing down end lots and package deals. You'll have to be sharp to turn
the tables on them, but you'll also find it an easier task because
there's no sales or store manager to appease and no corporate bottom
line to contend with. This section explores the Tools of the Flea
Market Bargain Hunter's Trade and how to use them.

[Die-hard bargain hunters check
out flea markets wherever their
travels take them.]

Local Color

If you've lived in your area for any length of time, chances are
that you know where your local swap meet or flea market is held.
But you might not know all of them. People who live in larger cities
and counties have access to a wide variety, some offering far better
wares than others. If you're new to your locale (or if you suspect you
don't know all the markets), the best way to find out is to ask—at
local antiques shops, among your neighbors or co-workers, and even
at the supermarket. You can also check the Yellow Pages and the
newspaper.

Die-hard bargain hunters who have the time make a point of
checking out flea markets wherever they happen to be—it's a fantastic way to soak up local color and seek out new and exciting deals.

Flea markets are traditionally held on weekends—in some areas,
every weekend of the year, in others once a month, and in still others
only two to four times a year. You'd be hard pressed to say that one

season is better than another for the flea market trade, but—as with the garage or yard sale—timing makes a definite difference.

X Marks The Spot

In some parts of the country, indoor emporiums run by a sole proprietor, brimming with junk and a few well-hidden collectibles, are also called flea markets. If you're willing to go through tables of the tawdry, you just might happen onto a lucky find.

Flea Market Finds

What can you expect to find at the flea market or swap meet? Some venues, like the Rose Bowl in Pasadena, California, and Brimfield, in Brimfield, Massachusetts, are renowned for antiques and collectibles. Others are devoted to cars, guns and knives, and even antique tractors and engines, but most play host to an incredible variety of goods, old and new.

You'll see everything from brand-new clothing and cosmetics to tools and toys, farmers' market-type fruits and vegetables to vitamins, houseplants, housewares, and even tires. Then there are the vintage wares—furniture, dishes, toys, 45-rpm records, books, and blankets. If you can name it, you can probably find it.

Like the garage sale, you can find a fair share of junk, too, but at swap meets it's more likely to be in the form of cheap toys, poor-quality clothing, and FIT crafts projects like crotcheted toilet-paper-holder dolls. What's FIT mean? Why, finger-in-throat. But sifting the chic from the chintzy is half the fun of the hunt, so get out there and get shopping!

Time Travels

Take time into consideration on your flea market travels. Vendors start the day before dawn so they'll be set up when the show opens, which can be as early as seven a.m. As with garage sales, if you're among the first on the spot, you've got first pick of all the best stuff. And that vendor won't be as inclined to haggle—he knows he's got a whole day of happy shoppers to sell to.

 The Bargain Hunter's [& Smart Consumer's] Field Guide

But if you're willing to take the risk that that ideal object may be snatched up by someone else, you can come back just before the market closes—close to four o'clock is good—and catch that vendor when he's tired and not looking forward to packing things up and hauling them home. That's the time to get the best deals.

Across A Crowded Flea Market

Which brings us to a topic of considerable controversy among the flea market set. If you find that perfect whosit—tea cart, tea dress, or tea rose print—and it's a steal but still more than you planned to spend, do you buy it or pass it by?

Some experts recommend snapping it up on the spot. A flea market is not like a retail store where there are several of the same item in inventory or more can be ordered from the manufacturer. In most cases it's a one-of-a-kind piece. And a once-in-a-lifetime deal. So unless it's going to break your bank, they contend, you should buy it without hesitation. Others suggest you leave it behind, shop the rest of the market and then decide. (A variation on the come-back-at-the-end-of-the-day ploy.)

We say there is no one right answer. You can tell that it's something that really speaks to you, as flea marketers say, (as opposed to those fleeting whims where you *think* you desperately want the thing but it's a passing mood) if you walk away and two aisles over it's still calling your name. Sometimes you'll know before you even leave the

Bringing Up Barbie

One of the best things about shopping for pre-owned merchandise is the possibility that what you fall in love with today might be worth a lot more in a few years—that it will become a valuable collectible.

While this is indeed possible, it's not a good idea to buy any tchotchke merely for its investment value—the market is too unpredictable. The general rule is that if you love an object and you can afford it, buy it. But if you're purchasing an item only because it *might* be worth money someday, put it back.

But what if you just can't resist the urge to stockpile and you want to start collecting something that will be worth a tidy sum in the next few decades? What should you choose?

"People tend to collect what they remember as a child between the ages of seven and 14," says Jim

continued on page 68

space. In that case, yes, buy it if you can. You won't be sorry.

If it's still speaking to you from across a crowded flea market, go back for it. Here's where you exercise your intuition, which gets better as you use it. If it seems that the dealer is getting a lot of action and that special item won't last long, hurry back and buy it. But if he seems to be having a slow day, you can shop the rest of the market and then go back when he'll hopefully be so delighted to see you that he'll lower the price. You can guess wrong, of course, but that's part of the thrill of the chase. And when your intuition's right, it's even more thrilling.

[Like gypsies of old, flea market vendors often travel from fair to fair.]

Tucker of the Antiques and Collectibles Dealers Association in Huntersville, North Carolina. "Add to that hobbies such as golf and fishing, things that relate to their work, and family things such as china, glass, etc. Glass has for many years been one of the top collectibles and remains as such. We don't see this changing, just maybe the type of glass. The younger generations seem to like to use what they collect instead of putting it on a shelf, so they are buying dinner and glassware of the '60s and '70s."

You Better Shop Around

Now, another of the things that makes flea market shopping exciting is that often that wonderful ware you just have to have is not the sole purview of one vendor. Because swap meeters often buy merchandise from wholesalers to resell to you, there can be more than one space with the same goods. So unless you're pretty sure it's a one-of-a-kind, shop around before plunking down your money—or you'll find the guy one aisle over is selling the same thing for less dough.

As a bit of contrary advice, don't count on that dealer being at the flea market again next weekend with the same wares. Vendors, like gypsies of old, often travel from one show to another, so you unless you ask you can't be sure where you'll find them. And because their merchandise is eclectic and often one-of-a-kind or one-closeout-of-a-kind, you can't be sure they'll have the same stuff next weekend.

Cool Kitsch

How do you know what's cool, what's kitschy, and what's just plain crummy? It all depends on you—your personal style, imagination, crafting capabilities, and comfort level.

* **That's not tacky, it's trendy.** If you're the type who can wear '50s pajamas in public and have people thinking they're the hottest trend in casual clothing, then the flea market is your personal playground. You'll have a ball with everything from bowling shirts to boxer shorts to those sequined cashmere sweaters Grandma wore and are now all the rage. But if you're more comfortable in jeans and t-shirts, don't buy the kitschy stuff. No matter how great a deal you get, if you can't feel good wearing it, it's not a good purchase. It'll only end up at the back of your closet.

* **Picture this.** It takes a certain amount of imagination to shop flea markets. When you browse designer home furnishings stores, for instance, you see carefully designed sets displaying color-coordinated furniture, accessories and silk plants. But at the flea market or swap meet, everything's in a jumble—antique mahogany dressers next to black plastic futons beside bevies of baby togs waving in the breeze. Practice the art of separating that potential piece from the background and seeing it for itself. Envision it in your home or office, complemented by the furnishings you already have. And don't worry that it won't match perfectly. It doesn't have to. Eclectic is in these days. A mix of time periods is cool, so trust your instincts.

* **Make it sew.** If you can wield a needle and thread, a paint brush, hot glue gun, or hammer, you can turn trash into treasure. Vintage fabrics from chenille bedspreads to nifty '50s-print tablecloths can become skirts or jackets, curtains, or throw pillows. A nicked and scratched piece of wood furniture can get a new lease on life with a coat of paint—and you can add decorative touches like hand-painted or stenciled accents for the latest in designer furnishings. All it takes is a hot-glue gun to transform ratty picture frames into shell-bedecked works of art, and a hammer, nails, and a shot of glue can remake that wobbly table into a sturdy work surface or dining zone.

✱ **Take comfort in your own abilities.** Lots of people have a fear of flea market flying. They think they don't have the ability to transform shabby into chic, or even so-so. Not! All it takes is a little training, a little practice, and a little self-confidence. And you can build all three.

Train yourself by browsing design and decorating books and magazines, watching decorating TV shows (turn to Home & Garden TV or Discovery Channel daytime for terrific tips), and window-shopping home furnishings at department and specialty stores and boutiques. Take a spin through model homes, which are often packed with clever decorating ideas. Decide what you like, what you don't, and what works and why.

For clothing rather than home furnishing fashion, follow the same game plan. Browse books and magazines, watch TV, and window-shop stores and specialty boutiques. Looking doesn't cost a dime!

Then practice. Buy a few items at garage sales and flea markets. If you go for low-priced goods, you can't make a major mistake. At worst, you'll have a good story and good fodder for your own garage sale, or for donating to charity. As you go, you'll discover that you have a better eye for design than you thought you did.

> [All it takes to turn shabby into chic is a little training, practice, and self-confidence.]

Salvage Central

Don't pass up old homes or buildings that are being razed or remodeled. You'll find architectural elements like fireplace surrounds and mantels, ornate carved woodwork from stairs and columns, stained or leaded glass windows, and ceramic tiles for the asking. You can also luck onto cabinets you can transplant directly into your own kitchen or bath, or use as extra storage space in the garage or laundry room. The best part? You can usually take away all you can carry so long as you remove it yourself. A word of caution: Never enter without first asking permission of the owner or contractor, and don't take without approval.

BUSINESS BEACON

Bargain Sampler

Use your business cards and resale certificate to get great bargains at apparel and gift trade shows, which are held throughout the year and around the country. (If you don't plan to resell the goods, you can still purchase them—just pay tax when you do.)

Wait until the end of the day or even the end of the show, when vendors are reluctant to lug their wares home; then neogiate great deals on samples.

Find trade shows by going to tsnn.com at (where else?) www.tsnn.com.

X Marks The Spot

Home builders offer potential buyers walk-throughs of exquisitely decorated models to show what their products can look like. But when the last house is sold, the model has to go—and all its furnishings and accessories, too. Find out when the model's scheduled to be dismantled and keep tabs, because you can often buy those pieces at terrific discounts. You win by taking home lovely items—the design company wins because they don't have to arrange to haul away, store, and then sell those barely used, but not new, goods.

Chapter Five
Attack Of The Antiques Lovers

OK, we've covered those quintessential shopping adventures for the hunter of previously-loved merchandise: the garage sale and the flea market. But that's not all there is. We've still got four terrific venues to explore: the auction, the antique shop, the estate sale, and the consignment shop.

Fair Warning

People who are die-hard antiques and collectibles shoppers—and good ones—often avoid the auction because it's an unknown. They equate "auction" with the loftier houses like Sotheby's or Christie's and think you can only participate if you're a blueblood with millions to spend on an Old Master. The truth, however, is that the socialite auction represents only a tiny fraction of the thousands that take place around the country every week—and a great portion of those are friendly, informal affairs that are held in country barns, tents, agriculture halls, and other eclectic meeting grounds.

Auctioneers take into account that their audience may be unfamiliar with the procedure and they explain as they go along. Since it's their job to get people in the mood to buy and keep the atmosphere "up," they're also good hosts, entertaining the crowd with jokes and patter amid the bid calling.

Miss Lila's Home Cooking

The country auction can be not only a great bargain site but a wonderful and absolutely free source of entertainment (providing of course that you don't buy anything). One of our favorites takes place once a month or so on Friday evenings in a small farming community about an hour north of our home. For no more than a couple gallons of gas and less than a $10 bill, we get a lovely moonlit drive through the countryside, a ringside seat at one of the best (and perhaps the only) shows in town, and stellar home-cooked food.

The auction takes place in the county agricultural center—which bears a striking resemblance to a junior high auditorium—and the 25 or so potential buyers perch on metal folding chairs around which are ringed the night's offerings. Off to one side, in the tiny kitchen, Miss Lila serves a selection of fantastic country cooking: home-made stew, meatloaf, and chicken-and-biscuits followed by Red Velvet cake, lemon meringue pie, and apple pie—your choice of dinner and dessert for $3.75. Trying duplicating that at any fast-food chain!

The highlight of the evening, of course, is the auction itself, which is conducted not by hifalutin' chaps with accents like Thurston Howell the Third, but by a comfortable, middle-aged auctioneer in overalls with a deep-South drawl and his assistants, two guys in jeans, t-shirts, and waist-length ponytails. When these two, who look like they couldn't hold a baby without dropping it, hawk delicate pieces of porcelain (and do it very well), it's entertainment in itself.

Treasure Chest Trivia

Auctions are one of the oldest ways on earth to buy and sell personal and real property. The earliest recorded auction was held in 500 B.C.

Wine and Crystal

Another of our favorite auctions comes to our town, much like a traveling circus, every three to six months. This one is much ritzier but even cheaper and just as much fun. It's held in the ballroom of a swanky resort hotel and features fine art, antiques, collectibles, and jewelry that the auction company brings up from various estates in South Florida.

Again the room is ringed with the goods on offer, but everything else is different. The auctioneer and his half dozen assistants wear suits, potential buyers sit beneath a huge crystal chandelier, and instead of country cookin', we're treated to complimentary wines, soft drinks, and hors d'oeuvres. But admission is still absolutely free

and you don't have to know anything more than how to have a good
time.

Tin Tubs And Tea Towels

What can you expect to find at an auction? That depends on what
type of auction you attend and where. Specialty auctions are held to
sell automobiles, real estate, livestock, farm equipment, commercial
and restaurant equipment, office supplies and equipment, manufacturers' inventory, and lots more. In fact, the manufacturer's auction is
where flea market vendors often find their wares.

At country auctions, you'll find the same sorts of goods you might
expect at a country flea market: collectibles like pottery, Depression
glass, and porcelain figurines; pine, oak, and walnut furniture; and all
those items so dear to the country collector's heart—old kitchen
utensils and farm implements, stoneware, soda bottles, tin washtubs,
and old tea towels.

At fine arts auctions, you'll find bronzes, art glass, art pottery,
teak and mahogany furniture, estate jewelry from diamond stick pins
to diamond-encrusted Rolexes, Oriental rugs, and original paintings,
lithographs, and prints.

And this isn't all. Half the fun of auctions is in the major mix of
merchandise—old and new, pristine and pretty banged up, originals,
reproductions, and even cobbled-together retreads.

Fertile Ground

So what makes the auction fertile ground for the bargain hunter?
One reason is that it's one of the best places to find antiques and
collectibles. People who own terrific treasures choose the auction as
the means to sell their stuff because they have a better chance of
selling it for a fair price. If they sell at a garage sale, they'll realize
pennies on the dollar and if they take it to an antiques dealer they're
likely to end up with only about 50 percent of an item's worth. (After

[Half the fun of auctions is in the major
mix of merchandise.]

all, the dealer has to make a living too, so he has to buy cheap in order to mark up enough to make a profitable sale.)

So the auction's a good choice. And because buyers tend to get excited and incite each other to higher bids, the price can rise significantly.

OK, we hear you saying, if the price goes *up* at an auction, what makes it valuable for the bargain hunter? For one thing, not a lot of people attend smaller auctions—in fact, a piece frequently will go up on the auction block and come back down again without a taker. So you might be the only bidder on something terrific, which means the price you set is the selling price.

There are regional tastes in auction objects as well as in fast food, so if you're savvy enough to spot something nobody in the audience is interested in, it's yours for the asking. We used to attend a weekly auction in Charleston, South Carolina, for instance, where rusty tin washtubs were all the rage. The bidding for these things, mostly among middle-class, middle-aged ladies, was fierce. But lovely silver tea services went begging, with the auctioneer removing them from the action unbid upon.

Sunday Drive

How do you find auctions? Check the classified ad section of your local newspaper. Auction ads not only provide a nice selection of current and upcoming events, but also list the types of wares on offer so you can decide whether that Sunday or moonlit drive will be worth the trip.

Once you get used to attending auctions you'll become familiar with the auctioneers in your area. Each has his or her own style in the types of merchandise they take on, its condition, the kind of crowds they attract, and what sorts of minimum pricing they set. So when you see their names in the advertisements, you'll have a pretty good idea of what to expect before you ever arrive (or even *if* you want to arrive).

You can also find auctioneers and auction houses listed in the Yellow Pages. Call and find out when and where their next events will be held. You can ask to be put on their mailing lists, although once you purchase a few items at auction the houses that have lists will automatically include you in mailings of upcoming functions.

X Marks The Spot

Look for auctions near you (or near a locale you'll be visiting) on the National Auctioneer's Association Web site at www.auctioneers.org.

Secrets for Auction Success

Capture those bargains and bid like a pro with our Secrets for Auction Success:

* **Check out the coming attractions.** Most auctions feature previews, in which everything for sale is placed on display well before the main attraction begins—usually an hour or two before the bidding opens. This is done just so that you, the buyer, can check out any items that catch your interest. You can pick them up and examine them as carefully as you like. The auction, like its cousins the yard sale and flea market, is a case of *let the buyer beware*—once you've bought it, it's yours. You can't return it later as you can in retail outlets. So it's up to you to give goods the once or even twice-over before the bidding begins.

* **Premium or unleaded.** Find out if the auction has a buyer's premium, a percentage (usually 10 percent and sometimes 15 percent) of the sale price that's added onto your final bill. If so, take the premium into consideration.

That, plus the tax, can increase that terrific bargain price considerably if you've purchased a high-ticket item.

* **Be an eager beaver.** Auctioneers usually put some of the best stuff up for bid first to get the crowd interested and excited. But people are often hesitant to start bidding—they're insecure of their abilities or waiting for someone else to set the pace. So if you arrive early and you're an eager beaver, ready to jump into the action, you can end up with some steals.

* **Be a late owl, too.** By the time an auction begins to wind down, everybody's tired. Many buyers have already called it a day or night and those who remain are likely to be on overwhelm and mentally trying to figure out how much they spent and why. So if you can stay perky and alert, you can glom onto great deals because the competition's pooped out.

* **Pray for rain.** If the weather's bad, the turnout will be too. So again, if you're an on-the-spot bargain hunter, you'll have the opportunity for some steals because the other bidders are at home watching TV.

* **Don't drink and bid.** It feels oh, so elegant to sit back and sip that fine wine while the bidding rolls along, but don't overindulge. If you get too into the spirits of the evening, you're liable to overbid. So keep it moderate, or stick to the sparkling water.

* **Chill out.** Half the fun of the auction is when the bidding starts going fast and furious. The audience gets excited and bids go higher and higher. This is good—for the auctioneer and the seller. But not for you. Decide during the preview phase, or at the very latest when the item comes up for bid, what your top bid limit will be and don't bid over that amount.

* **Keep an eye on the pros.** As you get used to auctions, you'll be able to spot the antiques dealers, just as you can at garage sales and flea markets. Watch them. It's a terrific way to learn what's worth buying and what isn't, as well as what are reasonable prices for those must-have pieces. The dealer, remember, isn't going to pay full retail because he has to mark up the price once he gets it to his shop. And

since you, as a savvy bargain hunter, don't want to pay
retail either, you can learn when to stop your bidding.

* **Don't be shy.** At larger functions, sit up close enough to the
stage so the auctioneer or his bid assistants can see you.

* **Slow it up.** If the bidding's going too fast on a piece you
want, you can sometimes slow it up enough to think out
your strategy. One way is to establish eye contact with the
auctioneer—let him know you're about to bid but are
considering the amount. The other is to change the bid
increments. If bidding is going from $100 to $200 to $300,
for instance, try making your next bid $350 instead of
$400. It throws off your competition and lowers the size of
the bid—and you can cut the increments again later if you
need to.

Expedition Tip

A few auction houses will arrange delivery of that sleeps-four
armoire or whatever it is you bought, but at most auctions it's your
responsibility to take your purchase away with you. So if you may be
buying furniture, either borrow your brother-in-law's pickup truck or
plan on driving home with table legs poking you in the back of the
head.

Expedition Tip

Make sure that auctioneer is licensed; he should advertise as such,
with his license number, and should be able to provide it if asked. In
the event you run into a problem, you can report him to your local
governing body, which may vary from state to state. (Contact your
city, county, or state department of revenue for more information.)

Selling The Estate

Estate sales are a sort of cross between the yard sale and the
auction. They're generally held when someone passes away and the

family decides to sell the belongings instead of divvying them up or giving them to charity. Estate sales are also sometimes held when a family moves and decides to start over fresh instead of lugging everything with them across country.

These events are generally held at the home of the deceased or the family that's moving. The action—like those murder mystery plays in which you're plopped into the thick of things—takes place in every room of the house as well as in the front and back yards. So if you've got an inveterate curiosity for investigating other people's homes, the estate sale is ideal for you because it marries bargain hunting with peeking into someone else's nooks and crannies.

X Marks The Spot

Get great discounts on everything from computers to cars to real estate at government auctions. Find local auctions by looking through your daily newspaper—you'll see occasional ads for city or county auctions of used equipment as well as police-impounded merchandise. For federal government auctions, go to www.firstgov.com .

When Ol' Blue Eyes Was Young

What can you expect to find at an estate sale? Lots of vintage treasures but not much that's new or late-model. A feature of estate sales is that they're held when the deceased was elderly—otherwise there would be some sort of immediate family like a spouse or kids to carry on in the home.

So you can find keen things, like Frank Sinatra albums dating from the days when Ol' Blue Eyes was young, in the living room; bottles of Avon perfume (in fragrances last made in the '50s), in the bathroom; and sewing patterns and fabrics for some long-forgotten sock hop or square dance in the spare bedroom. But unless it's an estate moving sale (and these are rare), don't look for Ricky Martin CDs or Doc Martens in the bedroom, because these aren't the sorts of things elderly people tend to buy.

You'll also find old and antique furniture, tools, lawn mowers, and other garden artifacts in the shed, and old magazines, Christmas ornaments, and books in the garage. Of course there are also kitchen utensils, small and large appliances, silverware, Tupperware, lifetimes of fine and also funky collectibles, vintage clothing, and linens. You can even buy the houseplants and potted geraniums!

Holding Court

You'll find estate sales the same way you find auctions—by checking the classified sections of local newspapers and perusing the Yellow Pages. If you can't find listings under "estate sales," try looking for auctioneers or auction houses. You'll also find estate sales as you make your yard sale rounds—the professionals who run these events take care to post directional signs at frequent intervals.

Some estate sales are run like tag sales. You wander around and when you find something you like, you bring it to the sale representative's attention and start negotiating a price. Other sales are run like regular auctions, with buyers standing around in the backyard and the auctioneer holding court beside the azalea bush.

Bargaining at estate sales is very much like bargaining at any other previously-loved merchandise outlet. You take the weather, the turnout, the time of day, and the general interest level of the participants into consideration, and open your negotiations.

continued on page 82

Careful! In America, *silver plate* means a coating of silver electroplated onto a base metal and is not as fine or expensive as sterling silver. But in England, *plate* means *sterling*. So if you happen to be in Britain or you're dealing with British goods, don't pass up the plate as second class.

Raiders of the Lost Consignment

If you're into previously-loved merchandise, yet another delightful avenue for bargain adventuring is the consignment store. This is a shop that accepts items from private parties and displays them for resale. When a piece sells, the store then splits the profits with the owner. So here again you have the opportunity to purchase one-of-a-kind valuables you'd be hard pressed to find down at the mall or at Wal-Mart.

But it gets better. The thing that makes consignment shopping a mecca for the bargain hunter is that at most stores, merchandise is marked down on a regular basis. Some go on a schedule of about 20 percent for every three weeks an item sits in the store. Others leave objects at a set price for the first 30 days they're in inventory, then mark down 10 percent a week. So if you spot a beauty of a butler's tray on a 20 percent plan, and it's priced at $150, you can wait. In three weeks or less (depending on how long it's already

reached out and grabbed us.

Except a boxed set of silver plate flatware. Most of the pieces were accounted for (which is often hard to find) the set was in excellent condition, and the pattern was attractive. But the price of $250 was not. We took it to the estate sales rep, who said he couldn't lower the price because the sale had only been in progress for half a day. He suggested we come back in the afternoon.

When we returned around four, he said he still couldn't lower the price because the sale had another day to run.

"We really don't want to come back again," we said pleasantly. " Can you work with us on this?"

The rep glanced around the room, where there wasn't much activity. "I could let you have it for $200."

"That's kind of steep," we countered. "It's missing several dinner forks and it's not a popular pattern."

continued on page 83

been in the store), it'll cost $120. Three weeks after that the price will be only $96. Then it'll go down to $76.80. How do you know when that great piece first came into the shop? The date will be marked on the sale tag or sticker.

You can add the thrill of gambling to all of this because you never know whether the piece will remain in the store while you wait for the price to go down or if someone else will come in while you're out of the picture and snap it up.

And there's another fillip of speculation, too: If a piece goes down to 50 percent of its original price and still doesn't sell, it doesn't get marked down again. Instead, the owner is called and asked to come pick the thing up. Or it gets donated to charity. So if you hesitate a tad too long, you lose.

[Consignment shopping combines gambling with bargain hunting.]

The rep gave another sigh. "How about $175?"

"We'd take it for $150," we said.

The man cheered up. "Done." He wrote up the sale, then started taking the silver out of the box.

We stopped him. "We need the box, too."

"Oh, I can't do that," the chap said. "It was just for display." When we subtly withdrew our credit card, the fellow relented. "I can let you have it for $40."

"Make it $20," we said, "and it's a deal."

And it was. We took the silver and the box, and left happy. Lest you think we left a miserable sales rep behind, he was smiling too. And his company regularly sends us mailings, inviting us back for another round of bargaining.

X Marks The Spot

Used furniture stores are wonderful places to shop. The selections—from swanky Thirties liquor cabinets to clunky metal office desks circa 1946 to red brocade couches that look like they came from a bordello—are so funky that just window-shopping is fun.

Furs To Furniture

What can you expect to find at the consignment store? It all depends on what type of shop you're visiting. You'll see everything from bridal gowns to maternity clothes, furs to furniture, plus sizes, baby togs, toys, computers, home accents, sporting goods, menswear, and more. Although many stores mix and match these categories, the most common varieties stock furniture or family and ladies' apparel.

Consignment furniture shops can play host to such diverse elements as a 200-year-old sideboard, a nifty Fities coffee table, and a two-year-young sofa. You'll also find antique and modern pictures and prints, Chinese cloisonné vases, silver tea sets, and lamps galore. Half the fun is that you never know from one day to the next what you'll discover when you walk in the door.

Consignment clothing shops tend to fall into two camps—the designer duds boutique, where only the best in haute couture is accepted for resale—names like Donna Karan, Anne Klein, and Oscar de la Renta—and the happy-go-lucky shop where cotton rompers nestle on a rack next to last season's jeans.

You'll also find hats, shoes, belts, and jewelry in among the clothing—and it's not at all unusual to find a designer dress with the price tags still attached, at a steal of a price. Consignment shopkeepers normally mark goods at about one-third to one-fourth of the original retail price—or less—depending on desirability and condition.

Treasure Chest Trivia

Recycled merchandise really is in! According to the National Association of Resale and Thrift Shops, resale is one of the fastest growing segments of the retail industry, with over 15,000 shops across the country.

The Bargain Hunter's [**& Smart Consumer's**] **Field Guide**

The Second Time Around

Where do you find consignment stores? Not at the mall, because the rent's too high. And not generally in the trendiest part of town, for the same reason. Most consignment stores are tucked away in small strip centers, but we've sometimes seen them in ritzy office areas and storefronts, cheek-to-cheek with upscale boutiques. Like the mercurial merchandise within, you never know where a consignment emporium might pop up.

The more affluent the neighborhood, the better the goods. You'll find fantastic, barely-worn designer togs in tony areas because people can afford to a) buy the garments in the first place, and b) cast them off for something new after they've worn them to a single party or a scant few meetings. People who live in modest areas, on the other hand, tend to buy their clothes at Wal-Mart or Kmart and can't afford to part with them until they're ready for the rag bag.

If you're not into a $2,000 party dress or a tux for $200, it still pays to look for consignment shops in upscale suburbs. You'll find terrific kids' clothes as well as plenty of fabulous "regular" stuff for the whole family at rock-bottom prices. (Four-dollar jeans are not uncommon, and neither are $5 shirts.)

The same rule holds true for furniture, toys, tools, and sporting goods. People in higher income areas yield better consignments than those on the other side of the tracks.

Keep your eyes open for consignment stores as you toddle around town. Don't be afraid to try them out. Recycling is hot these days. Eco-buying is in. And to paraphrase the old Frank Sinatra song, merchandise is lovelier the second time around.

Expedition Tip

Find truly stellar buys at It's A Wrap, a resale store in Burbank, California that purveys production clothing from nearby TV and movie studios. Not only do you get great deals on everything from t-shirts to designer duds, you get info on each tag about the studio and/or show your "new" (and some never even worn) clothes came from.

Treasure Chest Trivia

In case you thought the Goodwill store was all musty dark corners that nobody ever actually goes into—not. Goodwill's recent annual retail sales of donated goods came in at more than $941 million. Not bad, especially when you consider that you're helping people while you're buying.

The Formula Of Five

OK, so now you know all about the great deals to be found at consignment stores. But how do you determine whether to snap up that piece now while it's a great deal, or wait until it's a fabulous one? Follow the Formula of Five to get steals on consignment goods.

1. **Check the interest.** Ask if there's been much interest in the item. If it's caught your attention and no one else's, you can feel safer about playing the waiting game. But if lots of folks are making eyes at it, you might want to grab it while you can.
2. **History lesson.** Ask if the store has stocked similar items in the past, how fast they went, and what they ultimately sold for.
3. **Hello central.** If an item has been in the store for a while,

Emporiums of Gently-Used Goods

If a consignment shop is a recycled merchandise outlet and so are a thrift shop and a resale store, what's the difference? Good question.

While they're all emporiums of gently-used goods, and thus all resale stores, a thrift shop is run by a non-profit organization like the Goodwill, a children's hospital charity, or a church group. These stores usually get their merchandise through donations but they can also operate on a consignment basis.

Resale stores get their goods by purchasing them outright from private parties while consignment stores, as you know, try to sell someone else's property for a percentage of the sales price. Their inventory typically comes from individual owners but can also come from wholesalers.

ask the shopkeeper to call the consignor and find out if
she'll take a price lower than what it's currently marked
at. This strategy often works. Some consignors have
already told the store they'll take a certain percentage off.
Others, particularly if the object has been on the floor for
several weeks (and especially if it's a heavy piece of
furniture), would rather sell it cheap than have to come
pick it up.

4. **Take your pulse.** Get a reading on your emotional pulse in
the matter. How badly do you want the thing? If it really
speaks to you and you can afford to shell out those beans,
do so before it's gone. If, on the other hand, you can sail
out the door with nothing more on your mind than the
root beer float at the ice cream parlor next door, then you
can wait and see what happens.

5. **Trust yourself.** Go with your instincts. The more bargain
hunting you do, the better you'll get. So believe in
yourself!

Expedition Tip

Take advantage of Bargain Seeker's Secret No. 4 and make buddies
with the consignment store staff. Sign up for their mailing list—
you'll get sale notices, customer-only premiums, and other tips on
what's on the top of their resale stack.

Clothing Caveats

When you shop consignment or other resale clothing outlets, you
sometimes feel like you've hit a bargain bonanza. Everything is so
inexpensive it's hard not to buy up the whole place. But the savvy
bargain seeker shops wisely and doesn't get carried away, buying
simply for the sake of a sale price. Keep these caveats in mind:

* **The match test.** Consider whether that kicky skirt (or
  whatever) will match the other clothes in your closet. If
  not, it may not such a hot deal.
* **Dry clean decisions.** Look at the label. If it's something
  you'll wear often and it requires dry cleaning, you may end

up spending more on cleaning bills than you will on the garment itself. (Some "dry clean" items can be gently hand or machine laundered, but you don't know until you try, so be careful.)

* **Irregular inspection.** Some garments end up at the resale store because they're manufacturer's irregulars, meaning the cloth from which they were cut has a run or other textile flaw, they were cut on the bias (which means they twist instead of laying flat), or they're torn, stained, or the seams are crooked. In some cases these flaws are minor or can be easily disguised. In others, they ruin the garment. But you can get so excited about your find that your eye skips right over a major goof. Take a careful look before you get to the cash register and again when you place your find on the counter. If you ask, the salesperson will help you check over your finds.

* **Run a size check.** Shoppers don't always put things back in the right size section of clothes racks. Try checking a size or two up or down from your own for garments that should be in your sector.

Expedition Tip

In all pre-owned merchandise venues, be it garage sale, thrift shop, flea market, or consignment store, you'll find dusty boxes tucked into corners—things that have come in for inventory but haven't yet been unpacked. Be the first to investigate. The yuckier the box looks, the less interested anyone else is liable to be, and, often, the better the discovery. And if your find hasn't been tagged yet, you can frequently set your own price.

Antiques Alley

The antiques shop is a haven of pre-loved merchandise, a store that's by definition a resale extravaganza. You can find antiques dealers in every city and town, and in tiny hamlets out in the country. Some shops feature only fine antiques—high-priced objects bearing the patina of centuries of care. Others handle collectibles, bits and pieces of glass and brass, lunchboxes, hat boxes, cigar boxes, old postcards, old cookbooks, and well-used kitchen utensils. Still others specialize in garden gems, architectural artifacts, or vintage clocks.

Everything Old

Whatever the goods, just because it's called an antiques store doesn't mean everything in it is old. Many antique dealers sell reproductions, furniture that is crafted with care and of far better materials than the particle board stuff you assemble yourself from the discount store. But they're still reproductions. Reputable shops will mark the item as a reproduction right on the tag, so there's no question. Others take the attitude that if you don't ask, you don't need to know.

But it's not that simple. In the world of fine antiques, there are brand-new reproductions and old, or even antique, reproductions. In other words, you might find a 50-year-old highboy that's a reproduction of an 18th-century Chippendale. It's old but it's not an original.

If you like the piece, its age doesn't really matter. Except as far as price goes. A brand-new reproduction should go for less than a 100-year old reproduction, which in turn will be far less expensive than a 200-year-old one. But, a 50-year-old reproduction—not old enough to really count as an antique—can be less pricey than the brand-new piece. Go figure.

So you need to know what you're looking at. If you're not sure, ask. Most antiques dealers will cheerfully explain the piece to you. If they won't, you might want to take your business elsewhere.

How else do you learn? Information on antiques abounds. Take classes at local colleges and adult learning centers or from major antiques houses. Read books and magazines, and watch TV. The Home & Garden channel and PBS carry terrific programs that teach how to identify and appraise antiques.

Expedition Tip

Although you can find lots of fantastic buys on build-it-yourself furniture at the home improvement store or discount store, a vintage piece will hold its value far better. You can pass it down to your kids and even great-great-grandkids to enjoy, long after that particle-board piece has disintegrated.

Mall Mania

Inexperienced bargain hunters tend to get excited when they come across an antique mall, which features scads of small spaces owned by individual dealers all gathered under one roof. Hundreds of dealers! All those aisles of goodies! But in our experience, the antique mall is not always such a hot deal for the bargain-bound.

Why? One reason is that antique malls provide sales clerks, who aren't necessarily antique-savvy, as a part of the lease price for the space. So the dealers themselves are absentee shopkeepers. You can't ask questions about an item you might want to buy and you can't do any deep-down haggling.

The other reason is that dealers who display at antique malls often are inexperienced part-timers as opposed to the full-time commitment types who have their own shops and really know the business. So mall dealers, who often don't really have a feel for their wares, look up new acquisitions in a pricing guide and mark their tags accordingly. This is not a totally bad tactic (in fact, if you want to learn the antiques trade, it's a good idea to get your hands on a pricing guide yourself) but it doesn't take a lot of vagaries into account—the condition of the piece, regional tastes, and what the local market will bear. So their goods can be quite overpriced.

From L.A. To L.A.

How do we know all this? We used to have a space at an antiques mall ourselves. And we had a ball. There's nothing quite like having a legitimate reason to go out antiques-hunting. But we quickly discovered that a collectible that would easily fetch $25 in Southern California would gather dust for weeks in Northwest Florida even if you marked it down to $5. So although we were marking things at a reasonable price for L.A. (that's Los Angeles) and looking them up in *Kovel's Pricing Guide,* we couldn't *make* people buy them in L.A. (that's Lower Alabama/Northwest Florida).

Now, don't take any of this to mean that all antiques dealers at malls are inexperienced over-pricers, or that you shouldn't bother shopping the malls. You can have fun and, like in any other shopping spot on the planet, if you're a smart bargain seeker, you can steal some deals. The best way is to ask the sales help to call the dealer and find out if he'll take less. Often the answer will be yes—like the consignor, he's either weary of it sitting on the display floor or he's already left word at the sales desk that he'll take 10 to 20 percent under the marked price.

Prices on antiques can vary tremendously in different regions of the country. When you shop an area steeped in tradition and renowned for its history, such as the fine antiques boutiques in old Charleston, South Carolina, for instance, you'll find prices that are far higher than just across the bridge in suburban Mt. Pleasant. Don't pay higher just for the setting.

Mysteries Of The Tag Codes

Antiques dealers have their own secret codes—often right on the price tag—to tell them how they've priced each piece and how long it's been either gracing their showroom or collecting dust. If you can decode these cryptic labels, you'll know just how low she'll be willing to go. (This is will be easy if you're a pro at Wheel of Fortune):

1. **First you need to know how they do it.** A common method is to take 2 words that equal 10 letters, like M-O-N-E-Y T-A-L-K-S. Each letter stands in for a number one through 10. Like this:

   MONEY TALKS
   1 2 3 4 5 6 7 8 9 10

2. **This code tells the dealer how much she paid for the piece.** For instance, a tag marked MS means she spent $10 to put that item out on the floor. If you see something marked MSS, you can figure that S must be a 0 and she paid $100.

3. **If the item is priced between $150 and $300** and you see a 3-digit code with two matching end numbers, those two numbers are probably 55 or 00.

4. **You'll have to look at a lot of tags to break the code, but it can be done.** For instance, if you find a collectible priced at $10 and marked with an S, you can figure that

S is 5, because dealers often double the price of an object.

5. **Here's the Wheel of Fortune.** Now all you have to do is come up with two words that total 10 digits (no two letters the same) and you'll have broken the code.

6. **Codes also often contain numbers to remind the dealer of when the piece came into the store.** Sometimes it's an obvious date, like 033102 for March 31, 2002, and sometimes it's more cryptic, like the letter code used for the purchase price. So you might see something like this: MSS-NNMKK, which would be $155 on 3/31/99.

Once you've broken the code, what can you do with it? Use your knowledge as a negotiating tool. When you know what the dealer has invested, you can hazard a guess as to how much she can discount and still make a profit. And when you know how long it's been on display, you've got a good idea of how anxious she might be to see the last of it, at a lower price.

X Marks The Spot

Do a good deed for others as well as yourself by purchasing at charity auctions. You give your money to a worthy cause, and you can also get a tax write-off.

Chapter Six
Service Providers: Sidekicks In Savings

You can buy more than merchandise the bargain hunter's way—everything from plumbing to pest control, airline seats to a seat in the dentist's chair. It may sometimes feel as if you're at the mercy of the insurance company, the auto mechanic, and the plumber, but the answer is—not! Just as in shopping for tangible products, when you shop smart for services you're the one in the catbird seat.

Service providers want your business, and in most cases they're ready, willing, and able to work with you in order to get it. So just as you do with retailers, make bargain buddies and get steals of deals on all sorts of things you might never have dreamed possible.

Secrets Of The Service Techs

Need a plumber, gardener, or auto mechanic? You can bargain for their services—or for any other service provider's—just as you can with retailers. Now, obviously, you're not going to find a marked-down plumber sitting on the shelf, a demo gardener, or a display model auto mechanic, but you can still haggle.

No Worries, Mate

Finding a reliable and competent auto mechanic ranks right up there with one of the most-feared tasks in the life of the average American adult. When it's difficult to find a repair shop you can trust, who has the energy to think about bargaining? You do. As a savvy bargain hunter, you can accomplish both with, as the Aussies say, no worries, mate.

Grab that socket wrench and try these tips:

* **Lean into a learning curve.** Vocational and technical schools that train the auto mechanics of tomorrow are delighted to have patients to practice on—and they'll do it for free, or for a nominal fee. You get a professional job overseen by a skilled instructor; the students get the experience. Everybody wins! If your job's minor, you might even check it into a high school auto class.
* **Shop around.** For routine-type tasks like brake or shock installation or tire mounting and rotation, ya gotta shop around. Some repair centers will provide the installation for free if you buy the parts from them, but others won't. So make your calls first to find out.
* **Shop even more.** If you're taking your car in for major surgery and you don't already have a trusted mechanic, take it to two different shops for two different diagnoses. If they're both the same, you can go with the better price or the one you feel is a better shop. Or you can take the lower price to the better shop and ask them to match it. (What if the diagnoses don't match? Call around for a couple more opinions.)

Make Pals With The Mechanic

Your best bet for good old-fashioned haggling is to make friends with the mechanic. Not the grease monkey who's paid five bucks an hour to crawl under the car and look for oil drips but the guy who owns the shop or is the head mechanic. He's the one who knows what he's doing and he's the one you want tinkering under your hood. Talk to him in depth about your car and its problems, just as you'd talk fridges or computers with the department manager down at the retail store.

If you relax and let the mechanic be himself, you should be able to tell if he's honestly interested in your automotive baby or just greasing his palms, what his level of experience is, and what repair route he plans to take.

[Schools that train the mechanics of tomorrow will treat your car for a nominal fee or for free.]

Now you've found a mechanic you can trust and to whom you can return on a regular basis. And now you can haggle. Listen to his recommendations, ask what his price will be, then ask if he can do a little better. If the answer is no, press a little harder. Will it be less expensive if you provide the parts? Can he suggest any portion of the program that can be deferred for a short time so the whole expense doesn't come out of your pocket at once? Would it be better if you took your car to a specialist like the dealer or an import house for this particular problem?

The Painter In The Tuxedo

Along with the auto mechanic, the contractor and his colleagues the plumber, the electrician, and the painter are often perceived as dreaded folks who'll take your money, do a sloppy job, and leave with the work half-finished and you holding the proverbial bag. Not necessarily so.

We've seen our fair share of contractor crooks. But we've seen far more truly good guys who really are out there to make an honest living and help you while they're at it.

The best way to find an ace service tech—from the remodeling contractor right down to the lawn maintenance man—is the same way you find that marvel of a mechanic. Shop around, get a variety of estimates, ask for references (which you need to check—don't be one who doesn't bother), make buddies, and then start negotiating a price.

Keep these handy helps in mind as you go:

* **Do a background check**. Make sure that contractor has a license in your town or county. Call the building department and get the skinny—have they worked with him on many jobs? What's his reputation? You can also call the Better Business Bureau to see if any complaints have been filed.
* **Make sure he's covered.** Find out if he's got worker's compensation insurance and ask to see proof of the policy.
* **Give him the once-over.** Nobody expects the plumber or painter to appear in a tuxedo, but if he shows up in dirty, torn clothes driving a ratty, paint-splattered, rusty or dirty vehicle, he probably isn't going to take any better care of your job than he does of himself and his own belongings.

You can sometimes save money on lots of different services if you pitch in. Sometimes it's cheaper if you can provide labor on some types of home repair or landscape jobs. (You know this—you've watched Bob Vila!) Often, as you know, you can provide materials you've bargained for—from kitchen cabinets to ceramic floor tiles— and pay only for labor.

Dr. Bargainstone, I Presume

Contrary to popular thought, most doctors are real people. And especially in today's cutthroat world of HMOs and Medicare multi-regulations that take a lot of funds away from the physicians, medicos can easily empathize with your desire to keep a few pennies in your pocketbook.

Whether you're a doc or a patient, health-care costs in this country are all tangled up with the way insurance companies pay for services. So before we go any further, you need to understand how insurance companies pay for health care—even if you yourself are uninsured.

Many insurance plans (Medicare is just one example) set approved rates for various doctor and hospital visits and procedures. So let's say, for instance, you pop into your local medic for an electrocardio-gram (EKG). If your doctor *accepts assignment* from your insurance carrier, it means he'll take the amount the insurance plan has decided an EKG and the office visit to go with it is worth—let's make it $200. That's all he can bill.

But you probably also have a plan in which the insurance com-pany pays 80 percent, or $160, and you pay the other 20 percent, or $40.

Now, if your doctor doesn't accept assignment, meaning he doesn't want to take the insurance company's approved rate, he doesn't have to. He can charge you 15 percent above that if you've got Medicare, and more than that if you don't. Your insurance company, however, stickler that it is, will still only pay 80 percent of the approved amount. So now that $200 plus 15 percent is $230, and you're still responsible for 20 percent of it. So now you're paying $46 instead of $40.

What's Up, Doc?

OK, enough with the math. The point is that the price of your visit is often dependent on what kind of insurance you have and whether your doctor chooses to agree with their rates. If you don't have health insurance, you can potentially pay even more—not because your doctor is out to cheat you but because he's trying to earn a living for himself.

Look at it this way: If your doctor feels his EKG and office visit are worth $300, but he wants to help out his Medicare or other insurance patients, his hands are tied. He can't take more than $200 or $230. But he can charge his uninsured patients the whole $300—unless they bargain.

X Marks The Spot

One of the best places to shop for a variety of services is with the new kid on the block. Find a provider who's new in town or who's just set up shop—she'll be more likely to bargain because she needs the business. You get a discount; she gets a stellar reference! (If she's just come into town, check references in her previous location.)

Library Skills

Why spend big bucks on the latest spine-tingling suspense novel (or any other new book) when the library can provide it for free?

Krista Turner of Normal, Illinois, put her bargain-hunting skills to work to procure a copy of a hot new novel. Instead of heading to the bookstore, she took her request to the library. They didn't have the book in inventory, but not to worry.

Krista pointed out that the book was a kicky new release lots of library patrons would enjoy and convinced the staff to order it. Then she put her name on the request list. When it arrived at the library, she was the very first to read the brand new copy.

Here's how you do it, whether you've got insurance or not:

* **I'm pretty healthy.** *I don't plan on being in here much, so I'm never going to meet my deductible for this year. It would help me out if you let me pay what the insurance company would have paid and call it even.*
* **It looks like I'm going to be in here a lot.** *And it's going to cost me. It would help me out if you'd take the insurance company's portion as payment in full.*
* **I've done some research** *and I know that my insurance company pays more than most for any given procedure. So, Doc, I'd like you to do me a favor and take the amount my insurance company gives you as payment in full.*
* **I don't have health insurance.** *Can you charge me the same amount you'd charge someone who came in with Medicare? I'll pay you right now, which means you won't have to wait for payment like you would if I did have insurance.*

Another tactic is to use your sense of humor, as Rob did with our dentist back in the days when we were struggling writers.

* **I don't have any insurance.** *Can you give me the starving writer's discount?*

Our dentist's immediate response? **"Yes!"**

Expedition Tip

Just as at the retail store, cash is king. If you can pay your doctor or dentist immediately so he doesn't have to wait on the insurance company—which can drag its feet big time—then you're doing him a favor.

 The Bargain Hunter's [**& Smart Consumer's**] **Field Guide**

Do your bargaining with the doctor or dentist, not the nurse or assistant. The doc is the one with the authority in the office as well as the one who's ultimately providing the service.

Hold The X-Rays

Don't wait until after your doctor has worked his magic to start negotiating payments. Find out at the onset of a visit or procedure what your costs are likely to be, and then take it from there. As we said, doctors and dentists are human. If you're up-front with them, they'll help you out. Try something like this:

Gee, I can't afford full mouth x-rays on top of cleaning and fillings. Do you think we could just x-ray the part that's giving me trouble today and do the rest on my next visit?

You should never ask, or expect, that doctor or dentist to skimp on necessary procedures. But, just as you do with the department manager down at the home improvement warehouse or computer emporium, enlist him as an ally. If you treat him like a colleague instead of an omnipotent being and ask his advice with your financial as well as physical well-being, he'll appreciate you for it.

BARGAIN HUNTER'S JOURNAL
Two For The Price Of One

Jane Hogan of Panama City Beach, Florida had the misfortune to come down with a bad case of bronchitis while on vacation miles from home. She went to a doctor and at his request had chest x-rays taken, then had to schedule another visit so he could review the x-rays and suggest treatment.

When Jane returned home two months later, it was with another bad case of bronchitis. This time, knowing she'd have to get an x-ray and pay for two doctor visits— one pre- and one post-x-ray, she got the x-ray first and brought it with her. One visit, one doctor payment instead of two.

Save The E.R. For TV

Some people overspend on health-care by paying for more than what they need. Don't let this be you. Follow these Handy Health-Care Helps to save on doctor bills:

* **Save the E.R. for TV.** It's amazing how many people go to the emergency room for things like sore throats and tummy flus when they not only have to wait for hours to be seen but then pay through the nose. Check this out: To have the ER doctor do a Level 1 exam, a short evaluation to tell you that you have a cold and hand out a prescription, the hospital charges on the order of $94. And that doesn't include the doctor's bill, which can be another $40 or more. So you pay at least $134. On the other hand, you can go to a walk-in clinic and pay $70 to $80 for a first visit or $55 if you're a repeat patient. Or see your own doctor and pay $45. These fees, of course, have wide variations, but this should give you a good cost comparison. Bottom line: Save the emergency room for real emergencies.

* **Call your doctor instead of going in.** If you've seen your doctor or dentist several times for a chronic condition or have been in recently, you can often call and ask a question instead of paying a visit. The trick is to call in the morning, if you can, and call again if you haven't heard an answer by noon. Doctors are hard to pin down and their staff can't always grab hold long enough to ask your question. So if you call again it lights a fire under the receptionist or nurse and helps get a speedier response.

* **Ask your pharmacist.** Pharmacists are terrific sources for help with over-the-counter remedies for colds, flu, sore throats, rashes, and the like. They'll cheerfully help, either in the store or over the phone, and their advice is far cheaper than going to the doctor.

* **Let common sense be your guide.** All these helps are intended as tips for non-serious situations. But you should always let common sense be your guide. If you're dealing with something you're pretty certain is a simple case of sniffles or the 24-hour flu, fine. But don't let saving money stand in the way of seeking the proper medical attention for something that might be serious.

The Virtual Pharmacy

As long as we're at the virtual pharmacy, let's talk medications. Your pharmacist is another major health-care ally who often knows more about drug side effects and interactions than your doc does. Take advantage of her services with these Apothecary Advisors:

* **When you get a new prescription filled,** be sure to ask how you take it—with food, on an empty stomach, every how many hours, etc. It may seem like simple advice, but lots of people don't do it. And end up back at the emergency room or the doctor's office—or at home sick to their stomachs—because they took the right medication the wrong way.

* **Make sure, too, that you ask your pharmacist** to double check that your new prescription doesn't interact adversely with something you may already be taking. Otherwise, you pay for a prescription that you later learn you can't use.

* **In many cases, a generic drug is just as potent** and just as effective as the name brand. Ask your pharmacist's opinion, and if she says the generic is fine, go for it. You'll save a bundle.

* **Sometimes different strengths of the same drug** have far different costs. For instance, a 20-milligram pill can cost less than a 10-milligram one. Ask your pharmacist before she fills your bill if this might apply. If so, she may give you half as many of the larger dosage. Then you buy a nifty little device that cuts pills in half (cost: about $3) and take a half pill instead of a whole one. Savings: big.

Expedition Tip

When your doctor writes you a new prescription, ask if he's got free samples he can give you, too. (He often gets them from pharmaceutical company salesmen.) Try the samples and if they work, get the prescription filled. If you end up with an allergic or other adverse reaction, you find out before you've spent your pennies on the prescription.

Enigmas Of The Insurance World

Since we've dipped into the intricate world of health insurance, let's expand our coverage a bit and explore the enigmas of the auto insurance world. If you have a car, you know that insurance rates can vary widely, just as in the health-care arena. And while you can't do much in the way of deep-down haggling, you do hold some bargaining chips, and there are ways to get your rates down to the lowest possible level.

Find out from your insurance agent what discounts you may be eligible for. Some agents will offer these goodies when they write the policy. With others, you don't know unless you ask:

* **Not a chimney.** If you don't smoke, you can probably light up a tidy discount.
* **The fleet plan.** Many insurers will give you a package deal— a discount if you insure more than one vehicle with them.
* **Bonus for years of service.** You can often get a discount for having been a customer with the same company for a number of years.
* **Stellar student.** You may get a price break for being a full-time student.
* **Safe as houses.** Most insurance companies reward you with discounts for safety features like air bags, anti-lock brakes, and anti-theft systems.
* **Accident-free.** You'll also be rewarded for so many years of accident-free or minimal damage driving.
* **On the defense.** You may get a break for taking an approved defensive driving course.
* **More mature.** Auto insurers will often reduce your rate once you pass a magic age, like 21 or 25, because they figure you're now more mature and a safer driver. And you are, aren't you?
* **Just a Sunday driver.** If you have a van outfitted as a camper with stove, fridge, and beds and it's not your only set of wheels, ask your agent to write it up as a motor home. Since insurance companies figure these are driven infrequently, your rate will be lower.
* **The home office.** If you work at home, you can get a discount because you'll drive your vehicle less often than someone who has to commute every day.

Knock Wood

There are other subtle ways in which you can negotiate a rate with your insurance company. If you and your family are safe drivers and you don't—knock wood—anticipate accidents in your future, you may want to raise your deductible.

Why? The higher the deductible, the lower the premium. This could be a good idea if your car is elderly enough that in the event of an accident it wouldn't be worth repairing anyway, or if you feel financially secure about footing a bigger deductible in the event that fender-bender occurs.

Check to see what else you may be paying for with your premium. Some policies automatically provide towing services, but if you belong to an auto club like AAA or Good Sam's, you're double-covered. So you can cancel the "free" towing.

Old Betsy

One place it really pays to haggle with your insurance company is if you do have that heart-stopping accident. Especially if your car is a senior citizen and is totalled or badly damaged, the insurer may not want to pay you what Old Betsy was worth. But you can get them to cough it up. Here's what you do:

1. **Make it clear at the outset**—as soon as they tell you what they're planning to pay—that the amount is unacceptable.

2. **Don't let them send you a check** until you've agreed to the amount.

3. **Go on a fact-finding mission.** Look through your local newspaper, shopper, or Auto Trader and clip ads for cars of the same model and vintage as yours.

4. **Make copies** of these ads and send them to the claims department with a letter explaining that these demonstrate the current market value of your car, which is the amount you will accept.

This should be all it takes to do the trick. Once they see that you're a savvy negotiator, they'll see it your way as well. If not, let them know you'll be taking the matter to your state insurance commissioner.

Expedition Tip

It pays to bargain, but not to skimp. Make sure you've got the proper coverage for your situation and your family. Enlist your agent as an ally!

[Don't let the insurance company send you a settlement check until you've agreed on an amount.]

BUSINESS BEACON
Legal Eagle

You may consider your company attorney to be untouchable when it comes to bargaining. After all, attorneys seem to learn the steely-eyed, don't-mess-with-me bit in law school. But as a savvy bargain hunter, you can negotiate price breaks on routine filings and other legal matters.

Instead of keeping your lawyer at a distance, build a relationship and make him a part of your support team. Ask after his family; inquire about their doings. Express your appreciation for his services, not only by thanking him when you speak on the phone or in person, but by sending thank-you cards after the successful completion of more difficult and time-consuming projects.

Attorneys appreciate this more than you might imagine. Ours once told us that nobody bothers to extend thanks; that attorneys are consid-

continued on page 105

 The Bargain Hunter's [& Smart Consumer's] Field Guide

Master Or Mistress Of The MasterCard

Just about everybody has credit cards these days, and they're terrific—while you're shopping with them. But when it comes time to pay the bill you realize that that fun little plastic rectangle comes with plenty of strings attached. There's the interest and the finance charges and the annual fees—all sorts of charges tacked onto a bill you thought was only going to show your unfortunate lapse down at the CD & Chocolate Emporium.

As a bargain hunter, however, you can have the last word. You *can* haggle with credit card companies and save money. Follow along as we unlock the mysteries of the MasterCard (or Visa or Whatever card).

ered—like plumbers and dentists—crucial when needed and then best forgotten.

Your lawyer will also appreciate referrals; they're critical to the growth of his business. So when you refer others to him, he'll recognize your efforts and work even harder for you.

Pay your attorney's bills in a timely fashion (another thing many clients neglect to do); drop off a plate of cookies once in a while. Then ask for those price breaks—and get them!

The Huge Array

There's a huge array of credit card companies out there vying for your attention and your spending power—about 6,000 by recent count. That's a lot of plastic! And it gives you terrific bargaining power, so much that banks and other credit card merchants will work hard to give you what you want. In many cases, all you have to do is ask.

Let's say you've had a Third Planet BankCard for years. You're pretty happy with it. But here comes your latest bill, and as you read over the charges you see, right there after that great bargain you got on CDs and chocolates, the annual fee of $50. Well, you don't mind paying for the cool stuff you bought, but spending another $50 just to use this particular piece of plastic is not wonderful. So how do you get the credit card company to waive the annual fee?

Call and ask. Try something like this:

You: I've had a Third Planet card for years. And as you can see from my credit history, I'm a good payer. But I'm not happy with the annual fee on my statement. I'd like you to waive it.

Customer Service Representative: We'd be happy to do that for you. Just deduct the $50 from your statement.

And that's really the way it often works. Sometimes, however, you have to apply a tad more pressure. Like this:

Customer Service Rep: I'm sorry, but that's not our policy.

You: Then I'd like to cancel my card. I've got several others I can use that don't charge an annual fee, and I'll go with them instead.

Customer Rep: Let me see what I can do. Can you hold for just a moment? (She leaves you listening to the Muzak version of Rolling Stones hits, but comes back a minute or two later.) We'd be happy to waive that fee—for this year only. Just deduct the $50 from your statement.

Don't worry about the one-time-only routine. You can call again next year and do the same thing. And it will generally work then, too!

Good Interest Rate Hunting

Now let's look at another scenario. Let's say you've done some A-plus bargain hunting, you've found a cool package deal down at the office supply superstore—computer, printer, copier and scanner—all for one great price and you're about to head on over to lay your money on the line. It's a steal of a deal, but it's still a stretch, so you're going to put it on your credit card. Before you pay with plastic, however, you might want do some further bargain hunting—for the best interest rate.

Place a call to your credit card customer service center, and say something like this:

You: I'm planning on making a major purchase with my Third Planet card and I'd like to find out if you can give me a better interest rate than the one I've got now.

Customer Service Rep: We've got you at an 18 percent rate right now. How much were you planning on spending?

You: About $3,000.

Customer Rep: We've got a special program I can let you
have that would bring your interest rate down to 12 percent
for any purchases made over the next six months.
You: Is that the best you can do?
Customer Rep: I'm afraid it is.

Now at this point you've got three choices: a) You can take the
not-so-hot 12 percent and say thanks, b) you can say thanks-but-no
and try the same thing with another card, or c) you can try this:

You: I appreciate your help with this, but 12 percent isn't
going to work. May I speak to your supervisor?
Customer Rep: Yes, sir. (puts you hold)
Supervisor: How can I help you?
You: I'm planning on putting a sizable purchase on my Third
Planet card and I was hoping you could give me a better
interest rate. The representative I just talked with was
helpful, but couldn't do better than 12 percent. I'm sure you
can see from my record there that I'm a good customer, and
I'd rather spend my money with you than put it on my
Fourth Galaxy card. Can you help me out?
Supervisor: We could do a 9.9 percent permanent rate.
You: I just got a card offer in the mail promising 4.9 percent.
Can you match that?
Supervisor: I can do one or the other: 4.9 percent for six
months, which will then revert back to your current 18
percent. Or I can give you 9.9 percent unlimited.
You (thinking 'What's a card holder to do?'): I'd like it better
if you could do both.
Supervisor (banks love to have the last word): OK, we'll do
it, but you have to make your purchase within 48 hours.
You: That sounds perfect. Will it be in effect by the time I go
to make my purchase this afternoon?
Supervisor: I'll make the change to your account now.
You: Thank you!

So now you've not only got a fab deal on all that electronic
equipment, but you've also negotiated a bargain on those credit card
payments.

On The Titanic

What else can you deal on with the credit card people? How about getting them to waive a late charge or a finance charge—or both? You can! The secret again is just to ask. But you have to be a good guy or gal customer to begin with and have suffered an infrequent lapse. If you're the procrastinator type who's always late paying bills, this tactic won't do you any good. Assuming you are a good egg, however, here's how you handle it:

> **You:** I'm sitting at my desk, ready to write out a check for my current statement, but I noticed you Third Planet people have dinged me for a late charge and a finance charge for last month.
>
> **Customer Rep:** That's because we didn't receive your payment until the 29th and it was due on the 25th.
>
> **You:** I know. I had to go out of town unexpectedly and I didn't get back in time to put it in the mail. **OR** I've been working on a killer deadline project and, to be honest, I didn't mail it until the 24th. **OR** I know. I put your bill on my "do this now" stack and it got buried. **THEN YOU ADD** But I'm sure you can see from my record that I'm a good Third Planet customer and I usually pay right on time. Can you waive the late fee and the finance charge?
>
> **Customer Rep:** We'd be happy to do that for you. Just deduct those charges from your bill.
>
> **You:** Thank you!

It's that simple. You don't have to make up a melodramatic story about a death in the family on board the *Titanic*—the truth works fine. The only trick is that you do have to be a good customer. And of course, you can't use this technique very often.

King Midas Drools

You know all those fantastic credit card offers you get in the mail every week? The ones that promise a low, low introductory rate, no annual fee for the first year, and so many other freebies that King Midas would drool with envy? Look them over carefully before you decide to run with one.

First, that incredibly low rate only lasts for a few months—which can speed by faster than you'd believe possible—and then you're stuck with a card that carries the same rates as the ones you already have, or even higher.

Second, all those freebies sound spectacular—and they should. Some direct marketing expert toiled for hours to make them appear that way. But they probably aren't anything different than what your current cards offer. If you're not sure, call the ones you have and ask.

Third, some of those seemingly bargain-basement interest rate cards have a major flaw. (Your current cards may have the same one.) They may not grace you with a *grace period.* The grace period is the amount of time you have, generally 20 to 25 days, in which to pay the balance without incurring interest. If you don't have a grace period, you'll be charged interest on everything you buy from the minute you sign the charge slip.

And fourth, you can bargain with the card companies you already have. Call them up and tell them you've received this wonderful offer in the mail and you'd like them to match it or you may have to cancel their card and switch to the new one.

Treasure Chest Trivia

What's the difference between a credit card and a charge card? A *charge card*—like the venerable American Express card—lets you charge purchases but insists that you pay the balance in full when presented with the monthly statement. A *credit card* lets you charge those purchases and pay the balance off over time.

Too Many Cards Spoil The Broth

Having a small selection of credit cards to choose from in your wallet is a good idea. It gives you the bargaining power to cancel one if the company doesn't comply with your requests and still have another one or two on tap. But too many cards—like too many cooks—spoil the broth.

On a personal level, the more cards you have, the more you're likely to spend. And that's not being bargain savvy. Some experts recommend that you stick to one card per person or two per household (one for you and one for your significant other to each use as the primary account holder).

If you have a business, you'll want to use a third card for business purchases. It's far easier to track expenses when your company has its own card than trying to separate business from pleasure.

On a credit level, mortgage lenders and other picky types who decide if you're worthy enough for that loan look at credit cards not as proof that you're worthy of all that lovely credit, but as a scenario for disaster. In their eyes, each card and its available credit limit is an opportunity for you to embark on a spending frenzy.

If you've got 10 cards with available credit of $10,000 each, for instance, the mortgage company sees you suddenly buying $100,000 worth of goodies and then flying off to Tahiti, leaving them holding the bag on your house payments.

Bottom line: Don't be tempted by every tender offer that arrives in your mailbox.

Expedition Tip

Just because you've got several cards doesn't mean you should keep them all easily accessible—that's putting temptation in your own path. Choose one and stash the others in your safe or other not easily accessible spot. You can pull them out if you need them, but you won't have them on hand to spend with on a daily basis.

Bargain Air

Whether you're a footloose and fancy-free type who loves nothing better than to seek out new life and explore new (or old) civilizations or you're an armchair traveler for whom Sioux Falls is adventure enough, sooner or later you'll want to purchase airline tickets.

Talk about strange new worlds! The airline industry is fraught with intricacies, misconceptions, and misleading information, all designed with a seemingly single purpose: to thwart the bargain-minded voyager.

But not to worry. There are lots of ways for the travelin' man or woman to find terrific airline deals. You just have to know how and where to look.

The Cost Of Cauliflower

Airline fares are as changeable as an April breeze and less predictable. Carriers base their pricing on the ideal of having every seat on every flight filled, and to that end they're constantly tinkering with current rates. It's the equivalent of the supermarket bringing the cost of cauliflower up or down several times a week (or day), depending on how many heads have been sold in a given time period.

Try these high-flying tips for finding better fares:

* **Fly during the doldrums.** The traditional dead zones for airline travel are mid-week days or in the middle of the night. This is because most business travelers—the ones airlines love because they fly on money-is-no-object expense accounts—generally wing their way out of town on Mondays and return on Fridays. Saturdays are also doldrum days for airlines, so if you can make your travel week begin on Tuesday, Wednesday, or Saturday and end on a similar day, you can get a better price.

* **Take Saturday off.** Airlines will also give you a better price if you stay over on a Saturday for the same reason. They're banking on the fact that people who spend a Saturday out of town will usually return on a hard-to-book Sunday instead of on that easy-to-fill Monday.

* **Plan ahead.** Airlines will reward you for making your reservation at least three weeks in advance so they're assured at least that your seat or seats will be filled.

* **Go for the Big Bump.** If you're not in a hurry and you've brought a good book, get yourself bumped. All you do is show up at the departure gate with your ticket in hand and offer to stay behind in the event of overbooking. Monday mornings are ideal for this ploy, but you can do it any time—the worst that can happen is that you don't get bumped. And the best? By law, you get a refund of up to $200 off your original ticket price if the airline doesn't provide a replacement flight within an hour. Or—even better—you get coupons for freebie flight in the delightful future.

* **Avoid the hub.** You can sometimes negotiate a lower fare by flying into a smaller airport located near that big city you're aiming for, than by demanding the hub. Art, who

used to live in New York and work in Philadelphia, always
flew in and out of Newark, New Jersey, for a fraction of
the cost of using JFK in New York or Philadelphia International.

✳ **Don't think dinky.** Conversely, don't insist on a regional
airport that's too small to be serviced by more than a
couple of airlines. You'll pay extra big bucks for the
privilege of landing closer to home. Instead, extend your
travel plans and drive the distance to a larger 'port.

✳ **Keep asking.** Don't take the first price the ticket agent
quotes you. Ask if she can do better. Give her a hand by
being as flexible as possible with departure and destination
airports and dates, and keep revising your options until she
finds one that sounds palatable.

Expedition Tip

It's more fun to be mature! Many airlines give seniors age 62 (or
even, for some airlines, 55) discounts of 10 percent or more—or
coupon books for discount travel. Call or go online with the airline of
your choice and ask what programs are available.

The Bucket Shop

Another spiffy way to get cheap tickets is by going through a
consolidator. This is a company that arranges to buy up a bunch of
tickets from an airline at a wholesale price, then turns around and
sells those same tickets to you for a marginal mark-up over its cost.

In Britain, a consolidator is called a *bucket shop*. (Is this
strange? These are the same people who refer to waking you up in
the morning as "knocking you up.")

Once upon a time, consolidators were perceived as shady
operators because they undercut what used to be federally regulated rates. Now that things have been deregulated, some people
remain convinced that consolidators are on the slick side. Not!
Most consolidators are highly reputable companies, although a
few—as in any industry—can take your money and run. For

safety's sake, pay by credit card and check with the airline to make sure your flight's been booked.

Even with the most trustworthy consolidator, there is one way you can run into trouble: If the airline cancels or delays the flight, it won't put you up in style at a hotel or transfer you to another carrier as it would if you'd paid its retail price.

You'll find consolidators on the Internet, in the Yellow Pages under "Airlines, Wholesale Tickets," or in all those intriguing ads in the Sunday newspaper travel section.

X Marks The Spot

For absolutely free airline tickets, consider an *affinity* card. Many credit card issuers provide cards that give you points for dollars spent. When you reach a certain limit (usually 25,000 points, or $25,000 spent), you get an airline ticket to anywhere in the 48 contiguous states. Foreign travel requires more points (usually 65,000). You can put just about anything—even groceries—on your card, and as you know, it all adds up fast!

In With The Innkeeper

Most people rely on hotel chains' toll-free operators to give them the best rates. Not the savvy bargain traveler! As a bargain hunter, you should know the top secret of using hotel reservation systems: Don't rely on them. It's often best to go to the source and call the hotel itself. It's well worth that long-distance call to talk directly to the hostel's front desk people instead of to a reservations clerk who's possibly thousands of miles from the scene.

Hotel rates, like airline prices, bounce up and down with the head count. When there's a convention in town and everybody's just about booked solid, or when it's tourist season and the hotel's feeling flush, the rates are high. When things get slow, prices become extremely negotiable.

The 800-number clerk in Omaha, Nebraska, has no idea how many vacant rooms there are in Lake Oswego, Oregon, and probably doesn't care. And that's why you need to make that call directly. Follow these tips for getting a great rate:

* **Just ask.** Often that's all it takes. If you've been to the hostel before and gotten a special rate, let the desk clerk know and ask for the same rate again.
* **Name drop.** Most hotels and motels offer a 10 percent discount or more if you belong to the military, are a senior citizen, a member of the American Automobile Association, Sam's Club, or the Good Sam Club.
* **Go corporate.** You can often get a corporate rate for the asking. Be sure to bring your business card with you in case they ask to see it.
* **Prompt a little.** If you'll be arriving during a major off-season, prompt the desk clerk. Remind him that his occupancy rate will be low and you'll be helping him out.

Treasure Chest Trivia

The lodging industry term for the "regular" rate, the one you'll get quoted if you don't ask for better, is the *rack rate*.

Half Price For The Asking

Planning a trip to Atlanta, we decided to try a mid-price hotel near the convention center. So we called the chain's toll-free reservations number and told the representative we wanted a room for one month hence. The price: $120 per night. Then we asked if they were running any specials. Well, we were told, since we'd asked, they did happen to have a special discount rate of $63 per night. Wow! Half price, and all for the asking.

Then we called the front desk of a similar lodging in Marietta, a suburb about 15 minutes (when traffic isn't heavy) up the interstate. Their quoted price was $89, but when we reminded them that we'd stayed there two months earlier for only $54, they they gave us that rate again. Even better!

Chapter Seven
The Cyber Bargain Seeker

Up to this chapter, we've sort of skated past the world of e-commerce. But now it's time. If you're already an e-shopper, you'll find new tips and bargains in this chapter. If you're an online shopping newbie, you're in for a thrill.

Virtual bargain hunting is different from bargain seeking in a brick-and-mortar store. It has its own occasional frustrations, its own eccentricities, and its own very definite charms. And—warning—it can be every bit as addictive as bargain hunting in person.

So strap yourself into that cyber bargain seat (or desk chair), and let's go!

Zapped Into Cyberspace

A lot of people don't e-shop because they think there isn't anything more available on the World Wide Web than there is on Main Street. And these same people don't shop online because they also think that purchasing products over the Internet is unsafe—that their credit card information is going to be zapped out of cyberspace by hackers and used to buy the national debt's worth of who-knows-what. Not and not!

First, the amount of merchandise available on the Internet is astounding. You can shop many of the same stores and mail order houses that you find in the traditional shopping world—everything from Bloomingdale's to Montgomery Ward to Victoria's Secret—plus scazillions of Internet-only retailers you'd never find anywhere but online.

Second, shopping on the Internet is every bit as safe—perhaps even more so—than shopping at a traditional store. You do need to follow a few simple precautions, but this holds true for traditional purchasing methods, too.

For instance, you don't give your credit card number over the phone unless you know you're dealing with a reputable merchant or service provider. And you don't slap your credit card down on the checkout counter and walk away. (At least we hope you don't.) The same sorts of precautions are necessary when you e-shop. But we're getting ahead of ourselves.

Expedition Tip

A nice thing about shopping by credit card—online or off—is that you cannot legally be held responsible for charges of more than $50 made by someone who illegally uses your account. This is not, of course, an excuse to get sloppy with your card. You should also read the fine print that comes with the card, for example that you must report fraudulent purchases to the card issuer within 60 days of the charge being made.

The Shop Now! Key

Let's back up and take things from the top. First off, if you're a newbie, you're probably wondering how online shopping actually works. (If you're a pro-caliber surfer, you can skip this part.) We could give you all sorts of technical geek-type explanations, but that's like explaining that TVs work by intercepting carrier waves out of the ether when what you really wanted to know was how to turn the thing on and catch that old Jimmy Stewart movie on CineMax. You can find lots of terrific books that do a great job of explaining the techno-nerd stuff if you're interested—and you can buy them online.

Now, here's the "point me to the *shop now!* key" version:

1. **In place of a wallet with cash,** check, or credit card and a set of wheels or shoe leather to take you bargain hunting, you set out on your shopping expedition with this equipment:

* **A computer with a modem,** which gives you access to
  the Internet
* **An Internet service provider (ISP),** which connects
  you to the Net—in essence the way your telephone
  service connects you to worldwide phones
* **A Web browser like Netscape Navigator or Microsoft
  Internet Explorer** that lets you access the World Wide
  Web once you're online.
* **A credit card**
* **Your bargain-seeking radar**

Now, none of this stuff is complicated or hard to come
by. All recently-built computers come equipped with a
modem—if they don't, you can easily purchase one to add
on. New computers usually come pre-loaded with at least
one ISP (like America Online or EarthLink). If yours
doesn't, any one of the oodles of ISPs out there will be
delighted to sign you up. Ditto for Web browsers.

2. **Once you're online, you head for the "store" you want to
   explore.** For instance, if you want a good book, you go
   to Amazon.com, which bills itself (and rightly so) as the
   world's largest bookstore, with 2.5 million titles available. Read-aholic heaven! So you type in:
   www.amazon.com. Hit the enter key, and abracadabra!
   You're in.

3. **Go ahead—shop around.** Browse different categories,
   from cookbooks to mysteries to metaphysics, just as you
   would at the bookstore in the mall. Or type in the
   subject, title, or author of a book you'd like to look at,
   and Amazon.com takes you to it. You can look at the
   cover, read a synopsis and a review (and often an excerpt
   as well), peruse readers' comments, and get suggestions
   for other books by the same author or other books that
   people who bought this particular title purchased. Wow!
   Can you get all this at the mall store?

4. **When you find a book you want, you add it to your
   virtual shopping cart.** Then you shop on, adding as
   many books as you like.

5. **When you've exhausted either yourself or your virtual pocketbook,** you click on "proceed to checkout." Here you review your purchases, change quantities if you like (so you can buy two, one for you and one for your sister), or change your mind about a book and "put it back on the shelf."

6. **At the checkout "counter,"** you type in your name and address, your phone number, your e-mail address, your very own secret password, and your credit card number. You can also choose gift wrap and a message for the books you're sending to your sister, and add her address. And you choose the type of shipping you want: overnight, second day air, or ground transport.

7. **The checkout "person"** (sorry, no bizarre nail polish treatments to ponder or happy face/cherub/Halloween buttons to observe) totals your charges, adds tax and shipping and shows you the bill. If you're happy with what you see, you hit the *send* button and you're done. Those books are on their way!

8. **How do you know?** A short time later you get an e-mail confirming your order.

9. **A day or more later** (depending on availability and your shipping choice) you get another e-mail telling you your order's been shipped.

10. **Your doorbell rings.** It's the UPS man with your books!

Expedition Tip

Once you've given the Web site your personal credit card info and shipping address, you never have to do it again unless you change your address or the card you want to use. So every future purchase is quick and easy.

   The Bargain Hunter's [& Smart Consumer's] **Field Guide**

E-Shopping 101

Now, all cyberstores—and all brick-and-mortar stores—don't operate alike. They don't all offer the same departments or amenities such as product reviews or descriptions. But like brick-and-mortar shopping, the surprises are at least half the fun.

But back to e-shopping 101. You can see (we hope) why Internet bargain hunting is so much fun. Now let's explain why it's safe. Again, without going into techno-speak, when you send your credit card information through the Web, it's sent through a *secure server,* which *encrypts* it, turning it into long strings of coded numbers, letters and symbols (just like in a Ken Follett spy novel!).

So if the Hacker from Hades somehow tore himself away from trying to disrupt national security and concentrated instead on intercepting your Third Planet card—and then cracked into the secure server—all he'd get was a jumble of digits, letters and symbols.

So, take this simple quiz:

Which do you think is safer?
- a. Sending your card information over a secure server to an Internet store
- b. Giving your card information to a customer service rep at a mail order house by telephone
- c. Giving your actual card to the guy in the little window at the gas station, who has you sign the charge slip and then watches you drive away while he still has your card number and your signature in his hand

(Sorry, paranoid types, didn't mean to get you upset. But you do see our point.)

The major caveat here is that it's your responsibility to make sure the site you're shopping on has a secure server. If it doesn't, *don't give out your card number or any other personal information.* How do you know it's a secure site? Because it tells you, either in plain English or with an icon—a locked padlock—or both.

OK, now that you know how Internet shopping works and why it's safe, let's go bargain hunting!

X Marks The Spot

You don't have to travel to North Carolina's famous manufacturers' showrooms to buy quality furniture for your home or office. Buy direct via the Internet and get considerable discounts. Find participating manufacturers by going to a search engine such as Google (www.google.com) and typing in "North Carolina furniture ship direct."

Somewhere Out There

What can you expect to buy online? Let's revise that question. What can't you expect to buy? Here's a small sampling of what you can find: Airline tickets, baby food, computer stuff galore (this is after all computer shopping), hotel reservations, pet food, people food, and clothing. Antiques, collectibles, cars, trucks, and Hummers. Boats, bread, gift baskets, fragrances, furniture, and fine art. You can order a Maine potato sampler, hire a private investigator, clip coupons, and bid at auctions. New stuff, used stuff, vintage goods, and close-outs. If you can imagine it—and in many cases, even if you can't—it's somewhere out there.

Bargains Ho!

Shop the Web the same way you shop the swap meet or the retail store. Unless you know it's a steal that's going to be snapped up in a flash, you don't grab the first teddy bear you see in the first aisle. You hunt around, poking your nose into every nook, cranny, and cardboard box. You ask questions, get to know the layout of the store or flea market, and make buddies with the salespeople or dealers.

 The Bargain Hunter's [& Smart Consumer's] **Field Guide**

Virtual bargain seeking works the same way. You'll find some sites you'll fall in love with and others that will leave you cold, some that offer incredible deals, and others where the pickins are slim.

OK, we hear you asking, how do you make buddies and haggle when there's nobody to actually talk to? Isn't bargaining a two-way street?

One solution is to combine cyber-shopping with phone calls to live beings. We found, for instance, a software sale on the Parsons Technology Web site at www.parsonstech.com and picked out a title we liked. Then we called the Parsons people at the toll-free number and told the customer service rep which program we wanted.

When she asked if we'd like to order another title from their sale list, we asked if she could give us a better price on a clip art software package that wasn't on sale.

She gave us a 20 percent discount on the clip art and sent it to us along with the other program we'd ordered. So by bargaining on the phone for merchandise found online, we got two programs sale-priced for one shipping price.

[Combine cybershopping with phone calls to live beings.]

BUSINESS BEACON
Chaarge It!

Everybody loves credit cards. When you shop with them, you get both immediate gratification and deferred payment. And if you're traveling, you don't have to worry that your out-of-state check may not be accepted.

As a business owner, you should love credit cards too. Sure, when you accept them, you have to pay discount (interest) fees as well as monthly statement and transaction fees. But you also increase your earnings exponentially.

When you sign with a merchant card service, be a smart consumer and keep more of those earnings rather than give them away by purchasing your terminal instead of leasing it. Leasing sounds cheap—but it's not.

The card service will offer to lease a terminal to you, for instance, for $19 per month with no money down for 36 months. Which sounds

continued on page 122

Before you actually plunk down your money in a Web shopping spree, make sure the site gives a phone number to call in case you've got problems or questions—and of course, for further bargaining.

really inexpensive. But do the math: $19 times 36 is $684, which is a lot of money. Especially when you compare it to the purchase price of $300 for the same unit.

The card service may not even tell you you can buy that machine instead of leasing it unless you ask. So ask already!

The Virtual Shopping Bag

This brings us to another point about Web bargain hunting. Because you can't have that virtual sales clerk pop your purchase into a shopping bag and then take it home with you (hey, you're already *at* home), you have to arrange for shipping. And shipping charges can add up quickly.

Most e-shops give you a choice of shipping methods—the faster the delivery, the higher the charge. If you purchase several products at once (yes, you can bulk buy or make package deals), you save by paying one shipping charge instead of several.

Some Web merchants will give you options. If, for instance, you've ordered one item that's available immediately and another that has to be back-ordered, you can choose to wait for the back-ordered one and have them both shipped at the same time. Or you can have one delivered right away and then pay a separate charge to have the other one shipped later.

Free Stuff: The Next Generation

But Web shopping gets even better. There *are* some things you can buy and use immediately—without even waiting for shipping. Wish fulfillment of the highest kind! It doesn't work with purchasing pizza, perfume, or most other products, but if you want software or books and you really, really want them *now*, you can have them.

Go for *downloads*, which are offered by lots of software e-shops. All you do is pick out the title you want, pay for it, click a few keys, and wow! The software or book appears on your computer, ready to use!

Even better for the bargain seeker, you can find free software to download. Of course, it's not all going to be the latest version of popular game titles like Tomb Robbers In Space, but you can have your pick of some keen stuff:

* **Freeware** is just what it says, absolutely don't-pay-a-dime software that the developer makes available, often in the hopes that he'll catch the eye of that high-paying software publisher.

* **Shareware** is freeware: the next generation. You get to download the program for nothing, but after you've played with, er, *used* it for a specified period of time, you're expected to cough up the payment. If you're not nuts about it, you stop using it. Otherwise, every time you open it, a screen pops up that not-so-subtly reminds you of your obligation. When you pay, the developer gives you a secret software key that disables the *pay me* screen.

* **Demoware** is the third type of freebie software. Commercial developers (as opposed to the lone ranger techno-geek working alone in his basement laboratory) let you download programs to try out. The big difference between demoware and its siblings, free and shareware, is that demoware is basically a teaser. You get the program, but there's a catch, which is usually one of the following:

  * **You get all the features you'd find if you paid full price,** but you only get to use them for a period of time (typically 30 days) before the program disables itself.

  * **You can start and run the program a specified number of times** (usually 30 to 50) before it self-crashes. If so, make sure you access the program only when you'll have time to use it. If you spend only two minutes in it and then exit, you've still used up one free use.

  * **You get frustrated by limitations on what you can do.** This version is called *crippleware* because it cripples an important function like printing or saving, forcing you to either throw up your hands and disinherit the whole program or give in and buy the full-access version.

Expedition Tip

Whether you choose freeware, shareware or demoware, be *extremely* careful of what you're downloading and from whom. If you're indiscrimate, you could download nasty computer viruses along with the program, which can effectively crash your system and kill your hard drive. If you're not certain you're downloading from a secure source, don't do it. A freebie isn't worth blowing your system.

Read Online About It

It's not just software you can find free on the Internet. You'll also find online editions of scads of magazines and newspapers. Read your favorites without the subscription fee! Some are abbreviated editions, offering various articles, editorials and columns, but not everything you'd find in the paper version. (And of course you don't get those perfume ads with the sniffy-strips you can rub across your wrist.) Others carry a great deal of content. And most come complete with archives so you can rootle around in the back files without getting pesky newsprint on your fingers.

When you read online versions, you can't clip articles or tear out recipes, but you can easily print them. And you can access goodies you won't find in the paper versions, like virtual tours of homes in decorating magazines, chat rooms where you talk online to editors or guests, and the ability to send e-mail questions to experts.

continued on page 125

The Dusty Corners Of Cyberspace

Cybershopping is not just for new and reconditioned merchandise. You can find plenty of primo pre-loved items online. Like bargain seeking at your neighborhood garage sale or thrift shop, you can poke around in the dusty corners of cyberspace and come up with great stuff. You'll find pre-owned goods in two main places on the Web: the classifieds (just like in your hometown paper!) and the auction.

Classified Information

Bargain hunting in the online classifieds is just like sitting at your kitchen table with your morning java and the daily paper—with a twist. For starters, you'll find ads from all over the country (or even further afield), so

match it. His store policy dictates that they *will* price-match.

Even though the demo we had in hand was basically brand-new and was being compared to a reconditioned unit (which is still basically brand-new, but not quite), the manager cheerfully matched the reconditoned camera's price.

What was the bottom line? By combining e-shopping with traditional shopping, we got a cool digital camera for less than half price—and that's a pretty picture!

you're not restricted to goodies from your relatively immediate neighbors. Of course, if you find something you like, you can't hop in the car and go take a gander, either, but there are ways around that little obstacle.

For another twist, online classifieds often include a handy notification system that lets you know when the object of your affections comes up for sale. For instance, if you just have to have a 1963 G.I. Joe in full Marine battle dress, you tell the system what you want. Then, when an appropriate Joe makes the classifieds, you receive an e-mail alerting you to your man's appearance so you can buy him before somebody else does.

This is good! But what about the not-so-hot, the part about the fact that you might be in Lake Forest, California while Joe and his current owner are in Lake City, Florida? You communicate (you and the owner, not you and G.I. Joe), either by phone or e-mail, or both. You can have the owner give you a description of the action figure's condition or send you photos by snail mail (postal mail) or e-mail.

And with those finely tuned bargain hunter's antennae, you decide whether you want to give Joe a new home.

Auctions Away!

Online auctions work pretty much like up-close-and-personal ones, but not quite. Instead of walking into the barn or backyard or wherever the auction's being held, you wend your virtual way inside with your trusty keyboard and mouse. You nose around and see what's up for bid, just as you do at live auctions. But instead of items placed on tables under the trees, they're arranged by categories—antiques, books, collectibles, computers, jewelry, housewares, toys and more—and you click on whatever catches your fancy.

X Marks The Spot

As an online ads sampler, circle these spots: Classifieds2000 at http:/ /classifieds.excite.com and FreeClassifiedAds.com at www.freeclassifiedads.com (that's free ads, not free dads).

In Love With Lava Lamps

You might, for instance, choose dolls, so you click on Barbie. (You want to give your new G.I. Joe somebody to come home to after a hard day in the trenches.) You see listings of potential mates for Joe, with the starting bid price and other stats, like the number of bids thus far and the closing date for that particular auction.

(At the online auction house, each item or set of items is considered a separate auction with its own opening and closing dates and times. What do we mean by a set of items? Multiples of the same thing. For instance, a seller might have a dozen groovy lava lamps he's offering as one auction.)

When you find an item you think sounds intriguing, you click on it and are rewarded with a page devised by the seller, which includes a description of the product and sometimes a photograph. On eBay at www.ebay.com, you also get to read a mini-bio of the seller and view his photo (although not all sellers have submitted this info), and you also get to read comments from people who've bought something from him the past. It's like meeting a dealer at a flea market and having prior customers on hand to tell you if he's honest. And it's fun!

You're hooked. And you're ready to bid. (Having remembered that Barbie and Ken—not G.I. Joe—are an item, you've switched from the dolls category to collectibles and fallen in retro-love with the lava lamps.) But first you have to register, which means filling in all the little boxes with your name, e-mail address and the like that you go through when you buy anything else online for the first time.

At some auction sites you enter your credit card information while at others you don't. This is because at some online auctions the site itself owns the merchandise and you pay them directly. At others (and in our minds, these are the ones that are really fun), the site functions as the auctioneer, but you deal directly with the seller—just as you do when buying from an Internet classified ad. So the site doesn't need your credit card information because you don't pay it.

The Bid Babysitter

OK, so how exactly do you place your bid? Pretty much the way you do at a live auction, but again with a twist. You take a look at the minimum bid price (let's say it's $20 for a lava lamp print t-shirt), the bid increment (we'll make it $1), and the current high bid. Now, just as at the barn auction, if the current top bidder has upped the price to $30 and you don't think any t-shirt is worth that, you don't bid.

But you're a serious lava lamp aficionado (or about to become one), so you decide to bid. You enter your bid, the next guy enters his, and the race is on. And that's sort of all there is to it.

We say "sort of" because at a lot of auction sites, instead of bidding on a blow-by-blow basis, you enter your maximum bid. If you've decided that you're willing to cough up $45 for this particular volcanic beauty, that's the number you enter.

Now, here's the cool part: Once you've set your bid ceiling, you can toddle off and bid on other auctions, shop for a gift for your mom on a different Web site, or go outside and mow the lawn. The auction site takes over for you as a virtual bid babysitter.

If somebody else who's seriously into lava lamps comes along and bids $31, the site will automatically bid $32 on your behalf. If your arch rival ups the ante to $33, the site bids $34 for you—and so on until it reaches your top limit of $45. If at that point no one bids above you, you win the t-shirt and the site notifies you by e-mail.

But it gets even better: If nobody bids above that $34 you offered by the time the auction ends, you get the t-shirt for $34—even though you said you were willing to pay as much as $45. How's that for bargain power?

Expedition Tip

Just as at the "real" auction, if you're the winning bidder at a virtual auction, you're obligated to pay for the merchandise. Make sure the price you bid is one you and your wallet can live with.

Expedition Tip

Follow the same precautions for purchasing products at auction as you do when shopping the Internet classifieds. Never, ever send cash. Use a cashier's check or money order that can be traced if the seller claims he never received it. And if you're in doubt about his veracity or you're paying a goodly sum, use a COD or escrow service.

Going Dutch

You don't have to travel to Holland to participate in a Dutch auction. This type of online auction is put into play when a seller offers multiples of the same item—for instance, those hip lava lamps.

Here's how it works: The lamps are offered with a minimum bid of $40 each. You bid $50 for one lamp, another bidder offers $45 for one lamp, and a third bidder offers $42 for 10 lamps. (What's he going to do with them all? Who knows?) Now, you get your lamp for $42 even though you bid $50 because the lowest high bid was $42. And the other bidders—even the guy who wants 10—get them for $42 each, too.

[You don't have to travel to Holland to participate in a Dutch auction.]

 The Bargain Hunter's [& Smart Consumer's] **Field Guide**

CyberSkies

If you're contemplating a flight through those friendly skies, the Internet is the place to start. You'll find travel bargains galore, plus lots of sites that function as freewheeling journals from explorers all over the globe. Even if you end up going no further than from your desk to your favorite armchair (with your laptop at hand), you can experience some entertaining, informative, and even bizarre travel adventures.

X Marks The Spot

For travel reading that will whet your appetite for way cool adventuring, start off with Lonely Planet Online at www.lonelyplanet.com. To get your feet wet without the gonzo stuff, try the more traditional Fodor's Travel Service at www.fodors.com. (If you've noticed that these titles are remarkably similar to those guide books in the travel section of your local bookstore, you're right. And you can read them for free!)

Cents and Sensibilities

After you've read up on all those fab foreign climes (or maybe just New Jersey) and you want to hop aboard the next jet, you'll want to cybershop air fares. This is where you get to put yourself in the virtual travel agent's seat. Ready? Here's what you do:

1. **Click onto a travel booking site,** like one of these:
   * *Expedia* at expedia.msn.com
   * *Travelocity* at www.travelocity.com
   * *TravelWeb* at www.travelweb.com
2. **Some sites want you to sign up before they'll let you fare-surf,** but that's OK. You haven't bought anything you can't return, not yet anyway.
3. **Check fares.** All air fare sites work in basically the same way. You choose your departure and return destinations, the dates you want to travel, airline preference if any, and whether you want to wing it in coach or in luxurious first-class. Then, through the magic of cyberspace, you're presented with several suggested flights and fares. If you like one, you buy it.

4. **If you don't find one that suits,** you can stay on the same site and keep revising your options (dates, airlines and the like) until you hit the jackpot with a price that fits your pocketbook and your sensibilities.

5. **Keep in mind that you may not find a fare you like** on any one Web site. Despite the fact that every site claims it has unbeatable fares, you'll come up with a lot of fares so high they'll send your senses reeling.

6. **Not to worry.** Try another site. And then another if necessary. In the airline fare world, rates change at Concorde speed and can vary from site to site and day to day, or even hour to hour.

7. **When you find a rate you like, buy the ticket** in the same way you make any other online purchase. Print out your itinerary so you don't forget where you're going and when.

8. **A few days later the tickets are delivered to your door or mailbox** and you're off on an adventure!

X Marks The Spot

If you have the ability to travel at the drop of a hat, you can fly to exotic destinations for up to 85 percent off airline ticket prices and even for free (yes!) as a courier for reputable corporations. You're allowed only carry-on baggage, you generally must travel solo, and you must join a service that schedules trips (usually for less than $100 annually), but what a savings! For starters, check out Air Courier Travel at www.aircouriertravel.com. Find more companies by doing an Internet search on "air couriers."

X Marks The Spot

You can shop for hotel rate bargains the same way you shop for air fares, and on the same Web sites. But you can also check into Hotel Discounts at www.hoteldiscounts.com, which promises rates up to 70 percent off and even bookings for sold-out dates.

Fly You To The Moon

Yet another method for flying on the cheap is to go the ticket auction route. Besides providing you with rock-bottom fares, this shopping method is a hoot because it makes the airlines and travel agents match your price, instead of the other way around.

On the PriceLine site at www.priceline.com, you pre-shop for the best ticket price and choose the lowest one you can find. Then you post your own price and the bidding begins for an airline willing to match the rate you've set. The one that comes closest wins you as a passenger. And the whole thing takes only about an hour.

Don't imagine that you can fly to the moon (or even Half Moon Bay) for $5. The airline people aren't that desperate. You have to be reasonable—the PriceLine folks suggest you set a price that's an established low fare. But as a bargain seeker, you owe it to yourself to fly as cheaply as you can. Don't err on the over-reasonable side, either.

X Marks The Spot

Since the airlines live in mortal fear that they'll be caught with unfilled seats, you get the absolute best bargains by traveling at the drop of a ticket. If your schedule is flexible (or if you can twist it until it is), you can grab some great deals. Check out WebFlyer at www.webflyer.com and 1travel.com at www.1travel.com.

[By going the ticket auction route, airlines and travel agents match your price instead of the other way around.]

BARGAIN HUNTER'S JOURNAL

When You Gotta Go

We had to go to Los Angeles and we had to get there in four days. And we'd already flown our frequent flyer miles. But a dear and close family member had passed away and we wanted to be at the funeral. So, we put our bargain-hunting skills to work.

First we called the airlines and explained our situation. Airlines aren't completely heartless. They'll give you a special compassion discount if you've been bereaved or have a family emergency. You have to be prepared to show proof or at least provide the name of a priest, rabbi, or doctor—but this works. However, in this case the "special fare" of $1,680 per person from our home airport in northwest Florida seemed more astronomical than compassionate.

So, on to bargain travel tactic number two, the nearest big city or hub, which in our case is Atlanta. This time the special fare was $777 per person—a lucky number in Las Vegas, but not a bargain.

On to travel tactic number three: the Net. First we got onto Travelocity, touted as a supersaver site, and found fares from $1,038 on up. But hopping on over to Cheap Tickets.com, we found what we needed: round-trip fares to Los Angeles from Atlanta for only $238 each.

We cut our travel costs from the original toll-free telephone quote of $1,680 to an online rate of $238—a savings of $1,442 per person. Of course, we had to drive to Atlanta and back, but that was OK. We used the drive as a quiet time to remember Tim, a wonderful brother-in-law and a bargain hunter, too. We think he would have been pleased.

Chapter Eight
The Jewel In The Driveway

Treasure trove isn't always found on store shelves or in cardboard boxes at the back of the thrift shop. Sometimes it's out in the parking lot or the driveway. It can be a car, a van, a pickup truck, a sport-utility vehicle, or even a motor home. But whatever name it goes by and however many doors it has, it can be a honey or a headache, a lemon or a luscious deal.

Most people—even those who are ace bargain hunters at the mall or the flea market—view car buying with the same enthusiasm they reserve for the dentist or the IRS auditor. And with good reason. Car dealers have a well-deserved reputation for being manipulative, underhanded, sneaky, sleazy…. But let's be polite and just put it this way: They don't generally operate with your best interests at heart. So when the average American goes out to buy a car, he goes with the valid suspicion that he's about to be taken for a test drive of the sucker sort.

Purchasing a used vehicle from a private party is a car of another color—and another buying situation that makes most people blanch. How do you know you're getting a reliable vehicle and not a rust bucket primed to fall apart as soon as you get it home? How do you know what's a steal and what's not? And how do you negotiate?

Not to worry. The savvy bargain shopper sees an auto purchase as just another adventure. And that's just what it is—a terrific opportunity to exercise those haggling skills.

In this chapter, we'll show you how to fine-tune your expertise in the car buying arena, and we'll start with that arch-nemesis, the new car salesman.

So don your hard hat to protect you from flying dealer flak, buckle your seatbelt, and let's get car hunting!

The New Car Nemesis

Your best tools for dealing with the dealer are the **12 Secrets of the Bargain Seeker,** the same ones we've employed throughout this book. You mix in the car dealer's secrets, which we're about to divulge, and you're in the driver's seat.

Every Trick In The Book

Dealing with the car dealer is the bargain seeker's equivalent of hunting dangerous big game. In most of the retail world, sellers are genuinely nice people who want to help you get a good deal. So long as they make a buck, too, they're happy to work *with* you. But car salesmen are trained to work *against* you. These fellows are pros armed with every trick in the book to get you to buy at their price—and then pay some more.

So pull out **Bargain Seeker's Secret No. 1** and don't be shy, or in this case, intimidated. The bottom line of bargaining holds true on the car lot just as it does at the home improvement store or the flea market. The dealer needs you just as much—or more—than you need him. Those shiny vehicles are costing him money every day they sit on the lot, so when you go car shopping, you're giving that dealer an opportunity to move his merchandise. And you wield a tremendous amount of power merely by walking into the showroom.

Driving Diva

Buying a car is a major investment. Next to real estate, it's probably the second largest purchase you'll make, so this is not the time to be an impulse shopper. Apply **Bargain Seeker's Secret No. 5** and shop around.

Just like buying a TV or a refrigerator, you need to look at a lot of different makes and models and decide what you want. Besides the all-important question of price, think about features: 2-door or 4-door; convertible, sunroof or hardtop; automatic transmission or standard; 4-cylinder engine or V6? Decide what color you want. Are you a driving diva who'll be miserable unless you've got a stereo/CD player package with all the bells and whistles, or will you be happy with a radio and a tape deck? Narrow down your choices as much as possible until you arrive at the one you feel could be your auto soul mate.

Window-shop dealerships in your area. Take your time and snoop. It's OK to be a looky-loo. Climb behind the wheel. Sniff the leather. Get acquainted with the makes and models on offer.

Read all about it. Go to the bookstore, newsstand, or library and check out magazines like *Car and Driver, Consumer Reports,* and *Road & Track,* that offer reviews of new vehicles, and get the latest stats, facts, and figures on the models that interest you.

Expedition Tip

Don't forget **Bargain Seeker's Secret No. 4:** make buddies. It's hard to cozy up to a car dealer, but if you act cool (as in *cool and aloof* as well as in *hip and savvy*), you can pique his attention on your looky-loo forays and have him anxious for your return. Be careful, though! Make it clear you're just looking. Don't get roped into any discussions of pricing, trade-ins or any other monetary matters until the day you come back ready to buy.

Armed And Dangerous

When you've decided which vehicle is your dream creampuff— the one you're going to go for—do the last all-important piece of research and find out what the dealer's cost really is. Common knowledge has it that this information is so top secret not even the CIA has access to it. Not!

When you know where to look, it's easily available. Here's what you do:

* **If you have a computer, get online and go to Edmund's** at www.edmunds.com. Now look up the following for the vehicle you've chosen:

  * Manufacturer's Suggested Retail Price (MSRP)
  * Dealer invoice
  * Dealer holdback
  * Current incentives and rebates
  * MSRP of any options you'd like
  * Dealer invoice on those same options

* **Next, if you're planning on trading your present car,** you'll need to look up its trade-in value. If your vehicle is 10 years old or younger, you can find this information on the Edmund's Web site. If you're driving a senior citizen vehicle, you can find its trade-in value on the Kelley Blue Book site at www.kbb.com. You can also look it up in the N.A.D.A. (for National Automobile Dealers Association) Official Used Car Guide, which you can buy online or through your local bookseller.
* **If you don't have a computer,** find a friend who has one and will help you access this information, OR
* **Go to the library** and look up the new vehicle information in *Edmund's New Car Prices and Reviews, Edmund's New Truck Prices and Reviews,* or *The Consumer's Guide.*

Now you're armed and dangerous—at least to the dealer—because you know his secrets. You know how much that beauty sitting on his lot actually cost him and how much bargaining he can afford to do.

So let's take a look at the information you've obtained and see what it means:

* **Manufacturer's Suggested Retail Price,** otherwise known as the *MSRP* or *sticker price.* This is just what it says it is—the amount Ford or Chevy or Honda says is a "suggested" price—not a real price. All it really represents is a way for you to figure out the dealer's price.
* **MSRP on options.** Again, this is only a "suggested" price, not the real thing.
* **Dealer's invoice with options (if you've chosen any).** OK, now we're getting closer to what the dealer paid, but this isn't it, either. Why not? Because a lot of other items get factored in. Watch:
* **Dealer holdback.** In order for you to effectively use the holdback, you have to understand what it is: basically a refund from the manufacturer to the dealer. The dealer has to pay the manufacturer up front for any car he puts on his lot, but he gets a percentage of his money back when he sells the thing. How much? Anywhere from 2 percent to 3.5 percent of the MSRP, although a few manufacturers such as Volvo, pay a flat fee. A few others, like Audi and

Daewoo (don't ask us how to pronounce it), don't give holdbacks.

So if, for instance, the MSRP with your option package is $20,000, the dealer invoice with his version of the option package is $18,000, and the holdback is 3 percent, you know that the dealer gets $600 when he sells you the car (3 percent of $20,000). Now you take that $600 off the $18,000 invoice price, and the car is actually costing the dealer only $17,400. Pretty nifty, huh?

The holdback is a vital dealer secret, one that is often not even divulged to the salesmen. Why? Because if the salesmen don't know, the dealer doesn't have to share it as part of the commission.

But now you know, and now the big mystery of how car dealers can advertise big "blow-out" sales where they sell cars at factory invoice and still make a living is solved. Even if they do sell at invoice, they're earning hundreds of dollars per vehicle.

And there's still more:

✳ **Current incentives and rebates**. These are handed out by the manufacturer to encourage sales on less-popular models and come in two flavors: customer and dealer.

Customer rebates are about the same as the ones you get when you buy anything from software to brandy—you buy the product and the manufacturer gives you back a chunk of change. But in the vehicle arena, you can sometimes choose between a cash rebate and a lower finance rate. Rebates can typically range from $500 to $2,000.

With dealer incentives, there's also a choice involved: whether the dealer wants to give that cash rebate he gets for selling the car to you or hang on to it. If he doesn't have a lot of excess inventory to move—which may prompt him to advertise the incentive in another "blow-out" sale and pass the dough along to you—he can keep mum and keep the cash. This is another deep, dark dealer secret that the salesman may not be privy to either. And, in the dealer's mind, with good reason—those incentives can range from $500 to $5,500.

But *you* know, so you can subtract this off the dealer's invoice, too. So let's go back to that car with the MSRP of

$20,000. We've already knocked the price down to $17,400. Now let's take off another $2,000 for incentive, and we're close to the dealer's real, true cost of $15,400. Why do we say "close?" Because dealers often get still other perks in the form of additional incentives for moving certain models during particular periods, such as when the next year's models come out.

The Eleventh Hour

You feel better about car buying already, don't you? Good! Let's take a spin down to the dealership and see what other tricks the sales staff has hiding in the trunk. But first let's check the clock, the calendar, and the Weather Channel for the prime car shopping periods. Here's why:

* **End of the day.** The best time to hit the dealership is no more than an hour or two before it closes for the evening, when everybody from the sales manager to the lowest salesman to the finance-and-insurance person is exhausted from a hard day of harassing innocent buyers and is ready to call it a night. A car purchase is not a quick operation—maneuvering the customer from the first spark of interest to that signature on the dotted line can take hours, which salesmen use to wear down the would-be buyer. But if you show up late, you turn the tables. The longer the whole thing takes, the more concessions they'll be willing to make just to get you out the door and out of their hair, so they can go home.

* **End of the month.** Both salesmen and dealers often have quotas to fill that come due at the end of the month. If they sell so many vehicles or so many Humbug-VR4 models, for instance, they get a tidy bonus. So if you obligingly arrive at the eleventh hour on the 30th day (or even the 26th day or later), they may be more inclined to give you a bargain so they can add another notch to their belts and claim that bonus.

* **Stormy weather.** Bad weather doesn't bring in many shoppers, so salesmen are more willing to bargain with you. You're a warm body, and if they can't make a fortune off you, they can at least get points toward their quotas.

Talking Trade-In

OK, we've timed our mission perfectly. It's nine p.m. on a cold, rainy night during the last week in December. Or it's a hot, muggy, drizzly night at the end of July—your choice. And, hey, we still haven't done anything with that trade-in price you researched. Not to worry. We'll use it now.

At the showroom, the salesman will want to talk trade-in. This is because car dealers believe that customers are fixed on either a) a good trade-in price for old Betsy or b) a good deal on the new car. Once they've correctly identified you as an "a" or a "b," the rest is simple. They concede on the trade-in and nail you on the new price, or they offer you zippola for old Betsy and give in a tad on the new vehicle.

As a savvy bargain hunter, of course, you've done your homework. You know your car's trade-in price. They might try to tell you your mileage is too high or the equipment package doesn't qualify for a good trade-in price, or some other tale. But since you've already factored in these variables, you don't need to budge.

Expedition Tip

The worst time of the year for car dealers is the period just before and after Christmas. Shoppers are more interested in gifts they can fit under the tree than one that sits out in the driveway, and desperate dealers are anxious to actually make a deal.

Cherry Condition

Why is the dealer so anxious to give you a rock-bottom trade-in price? Because, of course, he's planning—like a good Ferengi—on making a profit on your car. He'll sell it at a dealers-only auction, sell it directly to another dealer, or sell it on his lot. And if he's planning on either of the first two options, he needs to buy it below wholesale in order to sell it at a wholesale price.

If he sells it on his lot to a consumer, he will, of course, get the retail price, which is far higher than the wholesale one. But it'll cost him more because he has to detail it inside and out, repair any mechanical glitches, get his body shop to bang out any dings, advertise it, pay a commission to the salesman who sells it, and arrange financing and insurance.

So if you can get the Kelley Blue Book trade-in or wholesale value for your wheels, you've accomplished something! The best way to do this is to leave as little as possible for the dealer to do. Bring it to the showroom in cherry condition. Clean all those fast-food wrappers out from under the seats, shampoo the upholstery and carpets, spritz it with car perfume. Wash and wax the exterior and buff up the tires with Armor-All.

When the salesman says, "I'm afraid we can't give you full price for your car because we'll have to do a lot of work to it," you bounce right back with "Did you look at the car?" and a full explanation of its great condition.

Expedition Tip

Look like a player when you go into the showroom. It's not necessary to dress as if you're having tea with the Queen, but your appearance should show that you can comfortably afford the car. Masquerading as a bag lady won't get you a better deal—all that will happen is that the salesman will dismiss you as not worth his time.

The Dealer's Arsensal

Car dealers are champs at getting you to pay more for that shiny new babe- or hunk-catcher than what you thought it cost when you started negotiating. So your job is not only to bargain down from the sticker price (the MSRP), but to avoid being sucked into paying up. Watch for these tactics in the dealer's arsenal:

* **The Go-Between.** Whenever you and the salesman negotiate a term in the deal, he has to go get the sales manager's approval. And the sales manager always says no, forcing you to concede some point. But while you think your friendly salesman has left you alone in that teeny cubicle because he's arguing on your behalf with the manager, he's really drinking coffee or filing his nails in the break room.

This is just a ruse to a) wear you down and b) make you think that in the end—when they've finally got you to agree to their terms—you've won, when you haven't.

Solution: Don't fall for it. Use all your bargaining skills and wear them down instead. One of the best tactics we've ever heard came from a listener who called in to the absolutely fabulous National Public Radio show, *Car Talk*. This brilliant bargainer reported that each time the sales staff presented her with a price, she said, "Gee, I don't know. I'll have to ask my husband." She'd use their phone to call Hubby at home, who would say into her ear, "That's a great price. Take it!" The bargainer would hang up and tell the car salesmen, "He says it's too much money." So they'd lower the price. She worked this scenario four times until she got them down $2,000 from the original price of the car. Sheer genius!

✳ **The Old Bait and Switch.** In this classic ploy, you walk into the dealership expecting to buy a car that was advertised on sale. But when you approach the salesman, you discover that, most unfortunately, somebody just bought the last one. Then you're steered into buying a more expensive model.

Solution: Leave. Not only are there other fish in the sea, there are other dealers in town.

✳ **We lost it.** Car salesmen figure the longer they've got you in their clutches, the more opportunity they have to wear you down, until eventually you'll agree to any price just to break free. So they frequently "lose" things. They may borrow your keys so they can check out your trade-in and then "misplace" them so you can't leave. Or they might ask for a deposit and then "lose" it so you can't get up in a huff and leave.

Solution: Don't give them anything to lose. If they want to appraise your car, go out to the parking lot with them. If they want a deposit, refuse to give them any money until everything's been agreed upon by all parties and you're ready to sign on the dotted line.

✳ **The Lowball.** This works pretty much like the bait and switch, except that the salesman quotes you a wonderfully lowball offer on your dream car and then, once he's got you twitching to get behind the wheel, he tells you that you don't qualify for that low price because of your credit rating, or they only had one left to sell at that price and it's been taken, or some other fibberoony. Then you're pressured into buying something more expensive.

Solution: Walk. Again, there are lots more dealers and lots more cars out there. You don't have to take this one.

Car salesmen have many more tricks at their disposal, including turning you over to a "closer," the sales manager or other salesman who'll give the negotiating screw a few more turns and see how much more he can wring out of you.

As an ace bargain hunter, you can avoid them all. Keep in mind **Bargain Seeker's Secret No. 7:** Be willing to walk away. This works better than just about anything at winning the new car game. If the dealer and his henchmen won't cooperate, leave. Don't worry— they'll follow you right out the door and beg you to come back.

Treasure Chest Trivia

Car dealers call a potential customer who leaves the lot, claiming she'll return to buy another day, a *be-back*. And it's automatically assumed she won't be back.

The F&I Office

Your bargaining work isn't done once you've finally come to trade-in and price agreements and you're out of the claustrophobic sales room. Next comes the F&I office, where the financing and insurance is arranged. Your absolute best bet is to get your financing somewhere else (at your credit union or bank) *before* you hit the showroom, so there's nothing for the dealer to negotiate. If you can't—or if the dealer's offering a special low-price finance package your bank can't match—then go for it. But keep your anti-bargain antennae on red alert, because you'll almost always pay more for dealer financing (traditionally about 2 percent) than you will for outside funds.

Don't buy any sort of credit insurance from the dealer. Those nifty-sounding packages—where they pay off the car loan if you're disabled or, as a movie Mafioso might say, become dead—will cost you lots more in the F&I office than they will if you purchase them from your insurance agent.

Don't drop your guard yet! The F&I office handles more than financing and insurance. This is where they try to talk you into all sorts of options that you either don't need or can get cheaper somewhere else. Rustproofing, under-coating, paint sealer, and fabric protection are unnecessary in today's new cars, and the dealer will charge you 80 percent to 90 percent above what they cost him.

If you want an anti-theft device, an upgraded sound system, or way cool pin-striping, check prices at outside sources before you go to the showroom. You're likely to find much better rates, so either go to one of those sources or get the dealer down to the same price.

Dealer prep charges are just what they claim to be—the *dealer's* prep charges. Don't pay his costs for him. And don't pay the *ADMU,* the additional dealer's markup that gets tacked onto certain sporty new models that are in high demand.

[Don't pay the car dealer's costs for him.]

Coming To Terms

When Karl Kopf of Panama City Beach, Florida walks into the dealership to buy a car, he comes out with a bargain. His strategy? He tells the salesman what he wants to pay, bottom-line—no ifs, ands, or buts. And he stands firm. If the salesman won't come to Karl's terms, Karl walks away.

During Karl's recent purchase, for instance, a shiny burgundy minivan, negotiations ground to a halt when the salesman refused to honor Karl's price.

"I told you what I wanted to pay and this isn't it," Karl told the fellow in no uncertain terms. "And then," he recounts, "I walked away. The salesman followed me, saying, 'Come in and we'll make a deal.'

"You make my deal or no deal at all," Karl told him. The fellow agreed. So they went back into

continued on page 144

Car Shopping Online

If you'd just as soon pass on all the fun and thrills of going head-to-head with the dealer but you still want a bargain on a new car, try shopping online. Several sites offer this service. You choose the make and model of the car you want, decide on an option package, and pick a snazzy paint color. Hey, this is fun! Then your dream car configuration is sent to dealers in your area who e-mail you with quotes. You print out the one you like, take it down to the dealer, and buy the car. Some sites even help you get all that nasty paperwork going so you spend as little time as possible at the dealership.

The beauty of these car buying systems is that since the dealer's provided you with a quote before you ever set foot on his showroom floor, the price-haggling portion has been excised. (Keep in mind, however, that you'll still have to be on your toes for add-on charges when you go to pick up the car.)

On most sites the service is free, but you are expected to be on your honor and not click the "get quote" button unless you're seriously interested in buying a car soon.

Some sites offer a dazzling array of car buyer's research in the form of articles, reports, photo spreads, stats, and side-by-side comparisons of various makes and models. Others offer financing and insurance links. Even if you're not in purchase mode, you can spend a lot of time road-surfing around in these sites, constructing virtual creampuffs. Not clicking that quote button is tough!

the office and the salesman wrote everything out—and then added $130 to the agreed-upon price.

"I see already you're figuring something different," Karl told him.

"That's just county taxes," the salesman said. "We can't ignore those."

"Yes, you can," Karl said firmly.

The salesman said he had to go consult with his manager.

"Don't ask him," Karl said, "I'm leaving." And he walked out. Again.

But he didn't have to go far. The salesman followed him out the door and begged him to come back—again. And then he wrote up a contract at Karl's price, including the county taxes. So Karl won the battle.

"It's a game you play," Karl says. "Most people just want the car so badly that they fall for it. You have to be strong—even if you like the car. Otherwise you don't get your price. The dealer usually comes around."

 The Bargain Hunter's [& Smart Consumer's] **Field Guide**

If you want to give Internet car shopping a spin, here are a few sites to get you started:

* **Auto-By-Tel** at www.autobytel.com
* **Cars@Cost** at www.carscost.com
* **MSN's Carpoint** at http://carpoint.msn.com

Over on the Priceline site at www.priceline.com, the folks who deliver the let-the-travel-agents-match-your-price auction concept for airline tickets have done the same thing with car buying. You choose a car, tell the site what price you want to pay or what sort of payments you'd care to make, and then submit your "bid." Priceline then goes to work finding a dealer who'll accept your terms with a smile and notifies you within one business day when it finds one who'll play.

If it's successful, you pay a $50 matchmaking fee. And if you don't show up at the dealership to claim your vehicle, your credit card gets dinged a $100 "good faith cancellation fee." If you decide to give this option a whirl, make sure you're serious.

Adoptable Autos

Not everybody can afford a new car. And not everybody wants a new car. Sometimes pre-owned (otherwise known as used) is a better option, for a variety of reasons. Price, of course, is a big one. A new car loses up to 50 percent of its value after its first birthday. So you actually get more for your money with a used vehicle.

Then there's the fact that, like computers, brand-new fancy-shmancy cars tend to have more bugs than models that have been around for a while. It's sometimes wiser to let somebody else deal with all the factory callbacks for that first year or so, and buy the car after it's cut its automotive teeth.

But best of all for the die-hard bargain hunter, shopping for a pre-owned, private-party vehicle is fun. It's like shopping garage sales and estate sales. You meet a lot of interesting, genuinely nice people, get a peek at neighborhoods you'd never otherwise have investigated (or even known existed), and have an opportunity to turn up that truly serendipitous, magical buy that you can keep forever—or sell later for more money.

Restoration Or Resurrection

Adoptable autos fall into one of these five categories:

* **Cream puff.** This is the one owned by that mythical little old lady from Pasadena—or the guy across town who's a perfectionist. Low mileage, no dents, no dings, immaculate inside and out, and meticulously maintained down to receipts for every oil change ever made.
* **Average Betsy.** This one's owned by your Average Joe. Not a vision in clear coat, but with no defects that can't be cured by a little TLC and the application of elbow grease. Probably needs a tune-up and a good detailing inside and out.
* **Fixer.** Here's a car that can be worth a lot if you're willing to spend a little to make it right. May need a paint job, for instance, or a new clutch, brakes, or a transmission. Use this defect as a bargaining chip.
* **Restoration.** The weekend project—the quintessential '63 Mustang that needs new upholstery, new paint, some mechanical work and industrial strength TLC, but has the potential to become a showpiece.
* **Resurrection.** The lifetime weekend project—only for die-hard car fanatics willing to spend years of Saturdays hunting down no-longer-manufactured parts and rebuilding from the ground up to recreate a classic.

The Zippy Speedster

The first stage of shopping for a pre-owned vehicle is similar to that of buying a new car from the dealer—you have to decide what you want and how much you're willing to pay. The easiest way to do this is to grab your local newspaper and your shopper publications and turn to the classified automobiles. Vehicles are usually categorized by type—classic, car, truck or van, and recreational vehicle—and by year. Take a look at the kind of car (or cars) you think you'd like and at different automotive years.

This will give you a quick guide to pricing in your area. If you had your heart set on a zippy red Speedster Sport Coupe, for example, but the ones in the paper are about $10,000 over your price range, you'll have to change your strategy:

a) **Choose** a car with a similar sporty feel that sells for a lot less.

b) **Hold out** for a Speedster that needs work.

c) **Wait** for one where the seller is desperate.

Keep in mind that you may wait a long time for options "b" or "c," so if you need wheels now, go with another make and model.

If there are only one or two ads for the car you want, check out the online classifieds or look up trade-in values in the Internet or library versions of the Kelley Blue Book. Why? Some people have highly inflated ideas of what their vehicle is worth. With only one ad to go by, you can't get a realistic idea of prices in your area (or anywhere else, either).

> [You may wait a long time for options "b" or "c."]

Leased Wheels

Unlike private-party consumers, businesses can sometimes benefit from leasing a vehicle instead of buying it. Why? You can write off all the payments as a business expense and don't have to worry about depreciation. Check with your accountant to make sure this plan can work for you.

You can use this perk to purchase a single set of wheels for your SOHO (small office/home office) company, or use it to lease a fleet of vehicles for yourself and your employees. And take advantage of bulk-buying bargaining power for both the cars and the insurance.

Expedition Tip

Don't wait until your present vehicle has gone to auto heaven to start shopping. You're in a much stronger position when you don't *have* to have new wheels immediately—you can afford to pick, choose, and haggle instead of taking the first thing that looks decent.

The Jewel In The Driveway

Runs Better Than It Looks

Aside from the information value, the car classifieds make entertaining reading. You can sometimes get a pretty good snapshot of the seller's mindset just by peeking between the lines.

One of our favorite ads read like this: *1989 Ford pickup. Runs better than it looks. $1,200.* You can see right away that this poor thing is probably a rattletrap that you don't want unless all you're looking for is a workhorse to haul hay or construction rubble. But you can also see that the seller doesn't harbor any illusions about his truck. He knows it's rough, so you can probably bargain your way to a nice deal.

Here's another of our all-time favorites: *1998 Honda del Sol, yellow, t-top. Excellent condition. $15,000 or better offer.* Why would this person think you'd offer more than he's asking? Who knows? Our advice would be to pass this one up as somebody who's expecting the moon.

Check out one more: *1994 Cadillac DeVille, 54,000 miles, excellent condition. Lady-driven. $10,000.* This one could be read (make that argued) two ways. If you're a macho "women don't belong behind the wheel" type, you might draw the conclusion that lady-driven is not a plus. This car will have had the brakes ridden down to the metal, never had its oil or transmission fluid checked, or have smushed bumpers from inexpert parallel parking.

If you're a lady driver, however, you can argue the opposite: that this car was probably treated with kid gloves. Its owner never burned rubber just to show off, never cruised at 110 mph just to see how it felt, and never hauled bags of cement in the back seat.

Sunday Driver

When you've identified a vehicle you like that's in your price range, it's time to place a call to the seller and pre-qualify the car. Asking the right questions over the phone can save you a lot of time and effort going out to look at real or figurative nonstarters. (And if all you want is a Sunday spin, it's not fair to waste the seller's time— go find a new car lot and bother the dealer instead.)

Use the list of questions we've provided below. Some of the answers may be given in the ad, but it never hurts to ask anyway, up close and personal. This will tell you if the seller is embroidering the truth about mileage, for instance, and can't remember what he put in the ad, or if there's been a typo in the ad (that Cadillac terrifically priced at $1,800 was actually supposed to be $18,000). And it can also be a springboard for further insights about the car. Most people are honest and are willing to tell you what you want to know. Once you get them started, you can have a great conversation.

Car Qualifier Checklist

- ❑ Asking price
- ❑ Number of miles on the odometer
- ❑ Automatic or standard transmission
- ❑ Exterior and interior color
- ❑ Overall condition:
  Does it have any rust?
  How's the upholstery?
  Any dents or dings? Has it ever been in an accident?
- ❑ Is it mechanically challenged? Ask about:
  Brakes
  Transmission
  Clutch
  Tires
  Does it leak or use oil?
- ❑ What kind of mileage does it get?
- ❑ What options does it have and how well do they function:
  Air conditioning
  Power windows, door locks, seats
  CD or cassette player
  Anti-theft system
  Cruise control
- ❑ Are you the original owner? This establishes what in fine art and antiques circles is called the *provenance.* You can assume that if the person is the original owner, he knows the car's history—if it's been involved in a wreck or suffered serious illness, like a blown engine or cracked head.
- ❑ Why are you selling? This will give you an idea whether there's some hidden problem. People usually sell a car for readily apparent reasons, such as a family addition that requires a larger or safer vehicle, an elderly or deceased family member who's no longer driving, or (usually in the case of a fairly new car) payments that are too high. You'll have to use your bargain hunter's antennae here, but if the reason for selling doesn't sound quite right, put yourself on

alert. "I can't afford to keep it up," for instance, is not the same as "I can't afford the payments," and could indicate that the upkeep (i.e., constant repairs) is an economic drain on the seller—and will be for you, too.

Honey Or Hellion

Once you've got these questions answered, you'll have an idea whether this car is worth further investigation. If it is, set up an appointment to view. Here's your excuse for that Sunday drive!

A lot of people dislike used car shopping because they feel they lack the skills to detect a lemon when it's squirting them in the face. It's true that you always run the risk of buying a bomb, but that can happen with a new car, too. In our experience—and we've bought a lot of pre-owned vehicles—most private-party sellers are genuinely honest folks who are as anxious to give you a good deal as you are to get one.

We're not mechanics and we don't profess to be. You should have any used car checked out by a reliable mechanic of your choice (not the seller's) before you hand over any money. But the following is a checklist of some things to look for on your pre-adoption visit that will help you ascertain whether you're looking at a honey or a hellion. These are the things we look for. You may have others. If you call your mechanic—that ally you've already enlisted—and tell him you'll be bringing the car to him if you like what you see, he may provide other pointers for you to watch for.

The seller should be more than happy to let you poke around to your heart's content. If for any reason he isn't, you've got a strong clue that something isn't right and it's probably wisest to thank him for his time and split.

Expedition Tip

Find out the wholesale and retail values of the car before you go take a look. It's one way to determine where to start bargaining if you decide you want it. You can go to the Kelley Blue Book or other car sites on the Net or check the information at your local library.

Car Inspection Checklist

- ❑ How does it look in overall appearance? Like a vehicle that's been well-cared for or one that's been sadly neglected?
- ❑ Take a peek at the odometer. What *is* the mileage?
- ❑ Check for flaws in the paint. This can be a clue to rust from the elements or dent repairs.
- ❑ Check out the upholstery. Is it torn or dirty beyond what a good shampoo can correct?
- ❑ Is the dashboard cracked?
- ❑ Look under the car. Are there fluids on the parking pad that could indicate an oil, radiator or transmission leak? (If it's summer and hot, you may see air conditioning runoff, which is OK.) Hunker down on your knees and peer under the car. Do you see rust or bends where the frame may have been repaired after a bad accident? Are there holes in the exhaust system?
- ❑ Check out the alignment of doors, trunk, hood, fenders and bumpers. If they don't line up well with the body, this is another indication of an accident that's tweaked the frame.
- ❑ Lift up the carpets and look to see if the metal is crinkled, another telltale of an accident.

Make sure the engine is cool before checking fluids or poking around inside. No burns, please!

- ❑ Check the oil level. If it's low, it could be that the seller isn't taking care of the car as he should. The color should be relatively clear, never black, unless the car is a diesel, which turns oil dark quickly.
- ❑ Take off the oil filler cap. Is it clean? Water residue or a milky white appearance indicates a motor problem.
- ❑ Check the transmission level. It should be at the proper level, a clear red in color, and should not smell burnt or feel gritty.
- ❑ Check all other fluids: power steering, brake, and clutch (if it's a manual transmission). They should all be fairly clear— sludge in any fluid means you'll need to have the car serviced soon.
- ❑ Look at the fan belts and water hoses. Do you see any hairline cracks? If so, it's not major but something that will need to be changed soon.

❑   How about that battery? Are the terminals corroded? You should be able to tell how old it is by the date on the top, which will have the year followed by a letter for the consecutive month (A for January, B for February, etc.)

❑   Peer at the tires. If they're worn you'll have to replace them. Uneven wear in front and back could indicate shock absorber or alignment problems.

❑   Have the seller start the car while you stand back and watch. Does it smoke?

❑   Does it start right up or cough to reluctant life?

❑   Does it run smoothly?

❑   Check all lights, turn signals, sound systems, and other electrical doodads, including any power windows, door locks, seats, sun roof, or convertible top. If it's a convertible, put the top up so you can check for tears.

❑   Test the air conditioning and heating.

❑   Ask the seller to let you see any and all maintenance records, log books, and owner's manuals.

Test Drive!

If you're fairly satisfied with what you see, ask to take that (hopeful) gem out for a test drive. Most people will cheerfully let you leave their driveway without them because a) they're honest and assume you are too, and b) your car is in the driveway or at the curb, so they figure you've got to come back for it.

Take note of the following:

*   Is it a good fit? If you're a petite person, can you reach the pedals? If you're tall, do you have enough head and leg room? Will you feel comfortable on that long drive to Vegas, or will you suffer a bad back or tush rot before you've gone 100 miles?

*   Does it pull to the left or right?

*   Do the brakes work well?

*   Does it shift through the gears smoothly?

*   Are all gauges—oil, water, temperature and gas—within normal ranges?

*   Does it make any strange or unusual noises?

*   Do you smell burning oil?

The One You've Been Waiting For

If you like the test drive, it's time to bargain. By the time you've gone through all this, the seller is probably fairly convinced—or trying to convince himself—that you're a player. Why else would you spend so much time on his car? He's hoping you'll offer to buy the vehicle and will probably be very disappointed if you don't. In other words, whether he realizes it or not, he's ready to negotiate.

Let's set up a little scenario to show you what to say. You've just test-driven the Speedster Sport Coupe you had your heart set on a couple of pages back. The seller is asking $7,000, which you know from your online research is exactly Kelley Blue Book wholesale. Retail is $10,000, so you knew when you saw the ad that, barring some horrible defect, it was a good deal. This is the one you've been waiting for.

It's an older model, but it's in pretty good shape. It needs new tires, a good detailing, and some minor mechanical work, all of which you figure will cost you a total of about $750.

The seller is anxious to make a deal because he's leaving for Europe in two weeks and he wants to get rid of everything before he goes so he can afford to rent an apartment in Paris. (Be sure to ask if he's having a moving sale.)

> **You:** I'm definitely interested in your car. You do have the title, right?
>
> **Seller:** Sure, it's on the kitchen table.
>
> **You:** Great. I'd like to give you $5,000 for the car.
>
> **Seller:** I already have it priced below retail. I'd be willing to come down a couple hundred, but not $2,000.
>
> **You:** I can appreciate that, but frankly, the car is not in perfect condition. It needs tires, a tune-up, a good detailing, and that's just what I see. I figure it's going to cost me at least $750 to get it in shape, and that's on top of the $5,000, which is really all I can afford to pay.
>
> **Seller:** I'd like to sell it to you, but $5,000 is just too low. I could come down to $6,500, but that's the best I can do.
>
> **You:** Gee, I'd like to meet you halfway but I'm still out the $750 to get the car in shape, and then I'll have to count in the money it'll cost me for sales tax, registration and licensing. That's another $600 to $700 right there.
>
> **Seller:** I really don't want to take less than $6,500.

You: I'd be willing to pay cash, which I have with me. (You discreetly reveal a roll of bills.)
Seller: How about $6,000?
You: That's still steep for me. I guess I'd better go. It was nice meeting you. Good luck with Paris. (You head toward your car at the curb.)
Seller (following you)**:** I'd like to give you the car. You seem like a nice person and it'd be nice not to have to deal with selling it any more. How about $5,500?
You: I could manage that much. I'd like to have my mechanic take a look at it tomorrow morning, and if he gives it the thumbs-up, I'll take it.
Seller: Cool!
You: Thank you!

Expedition Tip

When you buy that car, go over the title carefully. Check that the vehicle identification number (VIN) matches the one inside the windshield. Make sure the seller signs in the proper place and fills out any necessary fields. Motor vehicle department personnel can be extremely cranky about this sort of thing and it's no fun having to track down the seller after you've driven away with the car, especially if you or he lives out of—or leaves—town.

X Marks The Spot

If you prefer the no-haggle method of car buying, you can buy used cars online through most of the same sites that sell new vehicles. And if you like the face-to-face encounter, but don't see anything intriguing in your local paper and don't mind a drive to another area, try the online classified ads.

Chapter Nine
The Castle Keep

Being master or mistress of your own castle—or condo or split-level ranch—is part of the American dream. For most people, it's the biggest purchase of their lives and a giant step in terms of both spending power and financial debt, so it can be exhilarating as well as scary. (But since that pretty well describes life in general, you may as well enjoy the process.) How do you find a dream instead of a money pit? And how do you negotiate so it doesn't cost the proverbial arm, leg, and head of hair?

Not to worry. Purchasing that private castle or commercial property is like any other form of bargaining—it just takes more money and more patience. Property deals may sometimes be made in heaven ,but they're not generally made overnight. Which is a good thing. When you're spending a small fortune, you want the time to consider your strategy and think through your options. But whether your goal is to become a Trump-ette type mogul or just Majesty of your own keep, you can do it!

Estates And Keepers

Real estate purchases generally fall into one of five categories. Your strategy for shopping and for bargaining is the same, no matter which of these options is your goal. But it's important to decide which one you want—if you don't focus, if you're all over the hypothetical map, you can't do the research you need to find the right property and make that super deal. So as a very first step, choose a category:

* **The private estate.** The reason most people buy real estate: as a home base, a haven, a tax savings, a place to

decorate however you like without having to get the
landlord's permission, and of course, a castle where you—
and not your landlord—reign supreme.

* **The feudal estate.** Having your own home and earning
  money, too—by buying a duplex or other multifamily
  property that earns income from tenants, while you live in
  one of the units as the owner.

* **The turnover.** The property—distressed, neglected or
  ignored—that you buy to fix up, then turn around and sell
  to somebody else. (Some people live in these while work
  is going on, which can be either an adventure or a trial
  depending on how picky you are about drywall dust and
  the smell of paint, on how long you plan to take before
  turning it over, and on how often you want to move.)

* **The keeper.** Investment property you purchase to keep, not
  as a residence, but as an income-earner for the long haul.
  This can be, for instance, a single-family home that you
  rent out, a duplex or 4-plex you'll rent, or an entire
  apartment building.

* **The business.** If you're an entrepreneur, you may be
  looking for business property—a hotel, restaurant, office
  building, warehouse, or whatever suits (or can be made to
  suit) your needs.

Once you've decided on the type of property you want to buy, the
search is on. For the sake of expedience, we're going to refer to
everything as a house or home, but you'll use the same bargain
hunting techniques whether you're looking for a cozy condo for
yourself, an apartment building, a coffee bar, or a corner store.

Expedition Tip

Like buying a car, buying a house is easier if you don't absolutely
have to have one overnight. Start shopping when the need begins to
make itself known, not when you're up against the wall.

The Ultimate Rules

When you purchase that pair of jeans or jar of marmalade, you don't lose all that much if it turns out you goofed, but with property your investment is magnified by thousands. As with buying a car, doing the proper research is vital to getting a good deal. So heads up here, and learn the Three Ultimate Rules of Real Estate Shopping:

Rule No. 1: Know your market.

When you set out to purchase a piece of New York City or Northbrook, Illinois, or wherever it is you've targeted, you need to understand the market. Is real estate in that area in a slump or an all-time high? How long has it been that way? Are changes glimmering on the horizon?

If prices are depressed, you've got a good chance of picking up a bargain—but only if the market is about to make an about-face. There's no point in buying a little bungalow in an inner city community that's been on a downhill slide for years and shows no signs of turning around just because it's cheap.

But if you find a cute but neglected cottage in a low-priced urban area that shows all the earmarks of becoming a trendy district (new boutiques, coffee houses,, and bookstores are popping up, for instance, and hip young professionals are transforming fixers into fashion statements), then buy while prices are still low.

On the other hand, if there's a land boom in progress with everybody buying everything in sight, you can consider fair market value a steal. Don't expect to buy that same cottage for pennies after the neighborhood has completed its transformation and become *the* hot spot in the city. Land booms can happen out in the 'burbs, as well. If houses in the neighborhood you have your heart set on are snapped up as soon as they hit the market, you're not likely to find a bargain basement deal.

So how do you know what's hot and what's not? Ask your real estate broker or agent. A good one can give you an accurate picture of any neighborhood through his own knowledge of the area as well as through reports pulled from the multiple listing service. You can also determine a lot about a neighborhood through your bargain antennae and—if you've lived in the area for a number of years—through your own observational skills.

Rule No. 2: Location, location, location.

Any Realtor will tell you that location is everything—and it is. But a "good" location is different things to different people—and for different reasons. For you it might be an outlook on a golf course, which someone else might see as the peril of golf balls in their morning coffee. The big draw for you might be an outstanding school district for your kids, a breathtaking view, or proximity to your job. (Although we know of one prospective purchaser who turned down a well-priced bay view condo because she could see her workplace across the water and didn't want to have to look at it in her off hours.)

Obviously, some locations are going to be bigger perks to more people than others. You might like living across the street from the railroad tracks because you've always been a train fan, but most people aren't interested in having their house do the locomotion every time the 10:41 from Omaha speeds past.

Even if you think you're going to stay in the house you choose for the next 40 years, you probably won't. Lifestyles change along with age, family size, health, careers, and interests. So when you look at locations, consider not only what appeals to you but what will appeal to potential sellers somewhere down the time line.

If you can't afford a beachfront bungalow, a penthouse condo with a view of the city lights, or a mansion in Beverly Hills or Buckhead, you can still buy in an A-plus location. Choose a neighborhood where the residents have pride of ownership—where the lawns are trim, the houses freshly painted, and people have added landscaping, decorative mailboxes, outdoor lighting, custom windows or doors, or other features that tell you they're there to stay.

Treasure Chest Trivia

Levittown, New York, is widely regarded as the first tract home neighborhood in the country. Built in response to the post-World War II housing rush, former G.I.s, their wives, and baby boomlets could move into a two-bedroom, one-bath home with an attached carport for under $8,000.

Rule No. 3: Add value.

This is the rule with which your bargain hunting skills can really shine. Your ultimate goal in buying real estate—after scouting out a good location in a good market—is to locate a property where you can increase the value, just like when you buy damaged or demo merchandise at the retail store and make it sparkle. Find the worst house in the best neighborhood and get ready to make a deal.

As an ace bargain hunter, you've got an advantage over the average buyer. You've trained your eye and your mind to pick out the treasure among the trash. When you look for real estate, here's what you'll seek:

* **Curb appeal vs curb repel.** Houses often go begging for a buyer because they need a simple beauty makeover. Although there's nothing structurally wrong with them, they're multiple-listing wallflowers. They don't get shown by real estate agents and they certainly don't get buyers because they've got peeling, flaking paint, sagging screens and gutters, and ragged lawns. Or they're tidy enough but they've been painted in particularly gruesome shades of chartreuse and mustard by owners with a defective color sense.

    Most people lack the ability to look at a décor-challenged house and see it as it would look with these simple changes: fresh paint, new screens and gutters, a mowed lawn, and some flower beds. But you can, and therefore you've got a great chance at a great deal.

* **Outmoded original.** Some homes don't sell because they're old-fashioned—not in charming, vintage style but in a frumpy, outdated manner. They may have small, boxy rooms that are at odds with the open plans favored today, kitchen appliances that were trendy in 1974 but now appear antique, and bathroom fixtures that seem to have come straight from a downtown hotel for derelicts.

    Again, the average shopper can't look beyond these basically cosmetic flaws to the terrific bone structure underneath, so a house like this sits on the market without a taker. This one will take more work than its curb appeal-less cousin that only needs paint and some gardening, but if you're a handy man or woman or you can allocate the funds to hire out, you can knock out a few walls, replace fixtures, and own a charmer purchased at a bargain price.

* **Motivation plus.** If you're just not the fixer type—you end up with more paint on yourself than on the roller or the room, and you and the business end of the hammer always seem to end up in disagreeable encounters—you can still find a bargain. Scout out homes where the seller may be motivated to take a lower price: one that's fallen out of escrow in a previous sale, for instance, or where the seller has been transferred and is in a hurry to leave town. Unlike the other types of homes in this section, you can't identify the motivation-plus type on a drive-past, but you can ask your agent to be on the lookout. And you can look, too—you'll often see ads that say "motivated seller."

Expedition Tip

Don't confuse a fixer that needs only the renovation version of makeup or a nose job with the handyman horror that has structural defects. Falling foundations, perforated plumbing, bad wiring, and rotten roofing can add up to more woes than wonders.

The Genie In The Real Estate Jacket

Buying real estate is different from buying a pair of Reeboks or a refrigerator in one important aspect: the agent or broker. On most bargain adventures, you go one-on-one against the seller. But in property transactions, you choose a real estate agent to act as a liaison between you and the seller. This person plays a very important role in the entire process, acting as your negotiating proxy, expressing your ideas and emotions to the seller and his agent, and advising you along the way.

Some people believe an agent is an unnecessary part of the equation, and in some few cases this is true. But a good real estate broker can be well worth his or her commission, and unless you really understand the market, the neighborhood, the mechanics of the process, and the seller, your best bet is to cheerfully enlist the broker's assistance.

How do you find that genie in a real estate broker's jacket and build the kind of relationship that will bring you a super deal?

First you have to find the right one—an expert who knows the market in your town, and in the neighborhood you've targeted, inside and out. Who knows all the tricks of the trade, has been in real estate long enough to understand the fine points of negotiating deals with sellers and sellers' agents, and knows how to work with mortgage brokers and banks, escrow officers and appraisers. And one whose personality suits your own.

Not everybody's an expert just because they have a real estate license. There are lots and lots of agents out there who are at it part-time because it seems like a good way to earn extra money. But since these people aren't relying on real estate sales to earn their livelihood, chances are they haven't devoted enough time or attention to become experts. And an expert is what you want.

There are also an awful lot of real estate agents swimming around in the

continued on page 162

property pool who have neither ambition or imagination. Cross these folks off your dance card as well. Your dream agent must have the drive to help make your deals a reality and must have the vision to see what you see—the Cinderella beneath the flaking paint. If she can't, she won't be able to bargain with strength on your behalf.

The Top Producer

Now that you know what sort of agent you want on your team, how do you find her? Delve into those home buying publications like Homes & Land and dig out the Sunday real estate section. Reading through these will give you an inkling of who's hot and who's not. Agents pay for their own advertising (unless it's an office-wide ad paid by the broker), so the agents who have larger ads with more listings are most likely to be the major players in your town. Why? Because they've got enough sales to pay for the ads and because they're ambitious enough to get out there and push properties.

Reading through all these ads will also tell you which agents are the top producers, the ones who've sold millions of dollars in real estate in the past year. (Actually, it's not the ads but the agents who'll trumpet this news—real estate people aren't shy.)

Last, but definitely not least, you'll discover which top-selling agents work the neighborhoods you've targeted—another important criterion for your real estate ally.

The Appointment

After you've identified three or four of these top producers, call up the one that seems the best and tell her what you're looking for: the neighborhood, the type of property, and the amount you're willing to spend. Stress the fact that a beauty makeover or fixer is fine with you, if that's what you've decided on. Make an appointment to come into her office and go through the listings that she'll have chosen for you from the multiple listing service and printed out between now and then.

And you can tour model tract homes as often as you like.

The beauty of property window-shopping, of course, is that you never know when that serendipitous perfect house will appear. And since you'll have been researching the market all along, you'll recognize it and be ready to buy.

Once you get to her office and are scanning the listings, you can determine whether she's a keeper. Did she find the sort of properties you want? Are they in the right price range? Are they beauty makeovers or major surgeries? Do your personality and hers mesh? Quiz her about her background, experience, and recent sales. If she's the ally you're looking for, you're set.

But if she hasn't got the picture (and a lot of agents really don't listen to what you want), thank her for her time and go on to the next one on your list. Unless you live in a very small village, you'll have lots of agents to choose from, so don't feel limited to the first few and don't get discouraged. Keep working at it and you'll find that gem.

It's a good idea to tell each agent that you're interviewing several. This way nobody gets their feelings hurt by assumed "dealing behind the back," and the one who's really a go-getter will work to get your business.

Don't go out to view property with an agent you're not interested in, no matter how hard she tries to convince you. It's not only a waste of her time and yours, but it can become awkward if she shows you a property you decide to buy through a different agent a few weeks later. (Technically, your business on that property belongs to the first agent who shows it to you.)

What happens if you find the perfect property on your own without benefit of a broker or agent? Even if it's sporting somebody else's for-sale sign, your best bet is to call your own agent. Ask her to find out all the details and then arrange for you to view it.

If you don't yet have an agent, you've got a choice. If your bargain hunter's instincts tell you it's a hot property and requires quick action, go with the listing agent whose name is on the sign. If not, go with the same steps we've explored above—again so you don't get stuck with a drippy agent who can't or doesn't want to be a heavy haggler on your behalf.

Treasure Chest Trivia

In real estate lingo, a *FSBO* (pronounced fiz-bo with a long "o") is a house that's *for sale by owner*.

The majority of real estate agents belong to a *Multiple Listing Service (MLS)* that provides prices, locations, and descriptions of just about every property for sale in the area. Make sure the agent you choose is an MLS member—if she isn't, you'll lose access to hundreds of potential properties.

A kiss doesn't turn every frog into a handsome prince. In the real estate world, a FROG is a finished-room-over-garage.

Donning Your Deerstalker

OK, you've found the perfect ally agent and together you're going out to look at what just might be the perfect property. You'll want to do an on-site inspection, just as you do when you buy that pre-owned car, and you'll want to sound out the seller if he's home. Put on your mental Sherlock Holmes deerstalker and find out as much as you can before you get there—the more detective work you do, the better idea you'll have of what to expect and what especially to look for. Ask your agent these questions:

Broker Or Agent

What's the difference between a real estate broker and a real estate agent? A broker is an agent who has taken extra courses and undergone more extensive testing to become certified as a sort of "master agent." An agent has to work under a broker's supervision, but a broker can be a one-person office if she likes.

Some experts recommend working only with brokers, reasoning that their greater knowledge makes them more qualified to wheel and deal. Some brokers are indeed sharper than the average agent, but you can also find extremely qualified agents who are happy working under someone else's shingle and just haven't taken the time to go for the broker's license.

Don't take one or the other as a plus or a minus. Do your research and then decide which is the better ally for you.

✳   **How long has the property been on the market?** If it's been listed for a long time (and the market is not so depressed that this is the norm), there's a reason.

> ❁ The price could be unrealistically high, which could be a plus or a minus for you. If the seller is a stick-in-the-mud who's not particularly motivated, he's not likely to budge. But if he's getting really tired of having his house up for sale, you might be able to convince him to come down in price.
>
> ❁ The house could be cosmetically-challenged, so lacking in aesthetics that no one wants to make an offer. This is great for you!
>
> ❁ It could be a house of horrors with major structural defects that previous potential buyers have already discovered.
>
> ❁ It may have fallen out of escrow for reasons that had nothing to do with the seller, such as that the buyer got cold feet or couldn't obtain financing. And since people often spend their money, either figuratively or literally, before escrow has closed, the seller is probably mightily disappointed or has put himself in financial hot water (or both) and is in a frame of mind to accept another offer fast.

✳   **Has the house been shown a lot?** If the house has received a lot of attention but hasn't attracted a buyer, it's probably priced too high for the market. And again, the seller may have had just about enough of holding open houses and having to keep everything actually dusted all the time that he may be willing to lower his price—or he may insist on holding out. As with all bargain hunting, you won't know until you make an offer.

✳   **Have any previous offers been made?** Some agents may impart this information if you ask (providing of course that they know the answers); some may not. If you can find out, for instance, that the seller already turned down an offer for $10,000 under his asking price, you'll have an idea of how low you can go.

✽ **Why is the property being sold?** This is your best clue to the seller's motivation level. People sell homes for a variety of reasons that carry different amounts of negotiating weight.

> ❁ **Transferred out of the area.** This is often a good motivator. It's hard to buy a new house in a new town if you're still having to pay the mortgage on the existing place, so taking less money to get out quickly is a reasonable option.
>
> ❁ **Can't make the payments.** Sometimes people get in over their heads on home mortgages. When the bank starts muttering foreclosure, these folks will often decide that it's better to take what they can get and pay off the note fast than to hold out for a profit at the expense of losing everything.
>
> ❁ **Death in the family.** When an elderly parent passes on, the kids often don't want the house. It's easier to sell at a low price and be done with it than to hang on for months in the hopes of a few thousand dollars more.
>
> ❁ **Divorce.** Messy, but an unfortunate part of many modern lives. The bickering partners may decide to sell cheap to be rid of the house that's binding them together.
>
> ❁ **Change in family size.** Growing families and empty-nesters often decide to go for respectively larger or smaller digs. Because they're not pressured by circumstance to move quickly, they're usually not the best bet for bargaining— but you never know.
>
> ❁ **Already bought something else.** People often buy a new house before the old one sells. If it doesn't move as fast as they've figured, they find them-selves stuck with two mortgages—and often decide to sell for less to get out from under.

Fancy Vs Fixer

When you or your agent identify a potential property, have her pull up a list of *comps* (for comparables) from the multiple listing service. These comps will show everything in the neighborhood that's sold in the last year or two, along with square footages, number of bed and bathrooms, and both the asking and sales prices.

This will give you a good idea of how the house you're investigating is priced—low, fair, or high. But put your common sense into play. Just because another house of the same size and style in the same neighborhood sold for $150,000 doesn't mean the one you're looking at is worth $150,000. The one that just sold may have been tricked out with fresh paint, new carpet, French doors, the latest appliances, and other fancy features. This doesn't make the fixer you're going to view, with the flaking paint and the sagging screens, worth the same money.

But sellers whose neighbors have bragged about their sale price often believe they can attain the same monetary heights. Or their real estate agent, who's anxious for the listing, tells them what they want to hear. So keep your common sense in place, your bargain antennae tuned, and be prepared to negotiate.

Exterior Checklist

OK, you've grilled your agent—you know everything it's possible to know about the seller and his motivation—and you're pulling up in front of your prospective purchase. Don't take off that deerstalker! Now's the time to exercise all your deductive skills.

Be prepared to take notes as you go through the house, using the checklists we've provided below as well as anything else you see that strikes you. Just like when you buy a car, you'll use any negatives you see not only as "bewares" for potential problems but also as bargaining chips when you make your offer.

Keep in mind, too, that when you buy a house, you should have a qualified home inspector go over everything before you sign on the dotted line.

Now, check out these exterior factors as you make your grand entrance. After you've toured the inside, walk through the yard and around the outside to finish up your exterior checklist:

❑   How does the house stack up against its neighbors? If you're going for a fixer this doesn't really matter, because you can give it curb appeal. If you're not, take a careful look. Is it the

ugly duckling among the swans? Or is the whole neighbor
hood full of ugly ducklings? If so, tell your agent you're not
interested. (Location, remember, is a biggie—if the neighborhood is in bad shape it won't matter how many jewels you
bedeck your purchase in. Its value will always be low.)

❑ Is the house uncomfortably close to a school (lots of kids
running across the lawns and the sound of school buzzers
resounding throughout the day), a fire station (sirens at all
hours), a freeway overpass (vehicles rumbling past and
smoggy emissions), or an electrical substation that could be
the source of unhealthy electromagnetic fields?

❑ How does the house rate for curb appeal? A doggerino of a
fixer on the inside can still have a charming exterior. This is a
plus.

❑ How's the elevation? Is the house sitting in a hole that could
represent flooding problems every time it rains? Does it sit
above the crowd so water runs off instead of in, and so you
have a nice view, too?

❑ What about the approach? Does the house sit on a blind curve
so that every time you pull out of the driveway you risk
vehicular mayhem?

❑ Is there adequate street and off-street parking for your guests?

❑ Is the driveway cracked or pitted?

❑ Take a look at the roof. What kind of shape is it in? Is it
missing shingles or tiles, or just plain worn out? If the area is
prone to brush fires, is the roofing material fire-retardant?

❑ What is the pitch of the roof? As a rule of thumb, a builder
who spends the money to build a steeply pitched roof will
have lavished much more attention on the house as a whole
than one who slaps on a shallow-pitched one.

❑ What about the fascia, the woodwork just below the roof?
Does it show evidence of dry rot or water damage?

❑ Give the gutters a once-over. Are they falling off or non-
existent?

❑ Are the lawns and landscaping overgrown and unkempt?

❑ Is the yard full of junk that will need to be hauled away?

❑ Does foliage grow too close to the house?

❑ Do you see any cracks in the exterior walls that could indicate
foundation problems?

❑ What about retaining walls? Are they collapsing, or doing
their job?

❑ Check out any decks, stairs, or railings for signs of wood rot or sagging.

❑ If there's a pool, what shape is it in? Is it heated? What is the condition of the heater (if any) and pump?

Interior Checklist

Unless the neighborhood is bad or you've seen something to make you jump back into the car—like a caved-in roof or a minefield in the front yard—reserve your judgment. Keep your eyes open and your mental gears turning, because you've only just begun. Check out these interior factors:

❑ How's the floor plan? Is it open and friendly or boxy and choppy?

❑ Is the house dark and dreary or light and airy?

❑ Check out the ceilings. Are they low, making the house feel dark and cramped? Do you see water stains or other evidence of roof leaks?

❑ What is the condition of the flooring? Does it have carpets, hardwood, ceramic tile, or linoleum?

❑ Are there adequate electric outlets for each room?

❑ If the house is vintage, does it have circuit boxes or fuses that will need to be replaced?

❑ How's the plumbing? Check under sinks and around toilets for evidence of water damage.

❑ Is there central heat and air?

❑ Do you see cracks, bulges, or other evidence of foundation or settling problems in the walls?

❑ What appliances go with the house, and what shape are they in?

❑ If the seller is available, ask the following. If he isn't about, have your agent find out:

　❧ Are the air conditioning and heating adequate? What do the electric bills average?

　❧ Has the house suffered any fire, flood, or storm damage, and to what extent?

　❧ Is the house on city sewer, or septic? Have there been any main line problems? What condition is the septic system in and how often does it get cleaned? (Too frequent cleaning can indicate serious problems in the near future.)

❀ Is there a homeowners' association? What are the fees? Are any assessments due now or looming on the horizon?

❀ If the house is vintage, does it have an asbestos roof or flooring? (This can be a major cost to replace because of all the special precautions necessary to remove and dispose of asbestos.) Vintage homes (or even those built before 1978) can also have problems with lead-based paint, so keep this in mind as well.

❀ If the house has a view that makes it special, how secure is that view? Can someone build between the house and the scenery?

Swan Costs

If the owners are there, try to get a feel for the kind of people they are. Anxious or mellow? House-proud or couldn't care less? Easy to deal with or prickly?

And that's it. For starters. Now you'll want to go home and go over your notes. If you're not going the fixer route and everything seems to be in good shape, get ready to make your offer.

If you're looking at a fixer or ugly duckling, you'll need to determine how much it's going to cost you to turn it into a swan—just like we did with the pre-owned car in the last chapter. If you're not an experienced handy person, this can present some challenges. But don't despair. Here's what you do:

✳ **Make another appointment to view the house,** and this time bring along a friend, relative, or other ally who does have experience and will help you make pricing decisions. If you've already made buddies with plumbers, electricians, painters, or other contractor types whom you'd call in again for this house if you buy it, they'll often be happy to walk the job with you free of charge, or for a nominal fee. OR

✳ **Sit down with your list** and figure out what sorts of things you can reasonably expect to purchase at the home improvement store (appliances, kitchen cabinets, bathroom vanities). Now go shopping! Hit the stores and get prices on these items, then add them all up. The home improvement warehouse will be delighted to help you figure out your costs on materials and also on labor. (Figure in another 10 percent of your total material and labor cost as a contingency. No matter how well you calculate, there are always bound to be a few surprises.)

Playing The Game

Now that you know how much you'll need to spend, you can formulate your offer. Let's say the house is listed at $150,000. The seller has found a new job and has already moved out of state. He had the house sold once but it fell out of escrow and it's been back on the market for three months. You figure it needs $20,000 worth of work to make it a swan. That takes the price down to $130,000. But you're a bargain hunter, so you want to get the price down lower.

You instruct your agent to offer $100,000, explaining that you feel this is a reasonable offer because of all the defects, which you list. Some agents may balk at this technique, feeling that a lowball offer only insults the seller, who'll retaliate by demanding full price and nothing less, and refuse to negotiate. But we've purchased lots of properties this way and and we know you can usually work a deal. We've also sold lots of properties and had our share of "insulting" offers. You take it, leave it, or negotiate, but you don't get insulted. It's all part of the game.

Make sure when you construct your offer that you insert two very important contingencies:

1. **The sale must be subject to inspection.** You have the opportunity to come back with the home inspector of your choice (not the seller's) and meticulously go through the property. If you don't like anything in the inspector's report, you have the right to either renegotiate or rescind the contract. (Give yourself from three to 10 days from the date of the contract to have the house inspected, depending on how anxious you think the seller is.)

2. **The sale must be subject to you obtaining acceptable financing.** Your agent can help you word this section, but be sure it's in there.

Both of these contingencies will give you an invaluable out if the house turns out to be a horror or if financing becomes a nightmare.

Offer And Counter-Offer

The ideal scenario, of course, is that the seller immediately accepts your offer, the property passes inspection with flying colors, and the deal is done. But what's more likely is that the seller will come back (through his agent, who'll report to your agent, who will report to you) with a counter-offer of $120,000.

You can take it, figuring you've managed to get the house for $30,000 under the asking price. Or you can keep in mind the $20,000 you'll have to spend to make it right and counter the counter-offer. Since the seller has come down a sizable notch in price immediately, you can figure that he's desperate, so you might stick to your original offer of $100,000 and see if he bites. Or you might offer to split the difference between his price and yours and pay $110,000.

If he doesn't want to take this option—or if he's stuck fast on his original asking price—you can say thanks and go on to another property. Remember **Bargain Seeker's Secret No. 3:** Don't get attached. There are always other properties.

And just because the seller turned down your offer doesn't mean you can't try again. We've purchased two properties where the sellers turned down our original offers but later accepted them. In both cases the sellers were motivated—one because of a death and another because of divorce—and in both cases offers that were accepted after ours fell out of escrow. So when we learned the properties were on the market again, we came back with the same lowballs. And had them accepted immediately!

So if at first you don't succeed—and you don't find something you like just as well or better in the meantime—have your agent keep an eye out. If that property is still on the market in another few weeks or a month, make another offer. The worst that can happen is that it will be rejected. The best is that you win the house.

X Marks The Spot

Buy your dream home directly from the bank. You can often work out incredible terms with very little fuss on foreclosures. The bank needs to get these houses off their books and will work with you to get you into the property. To find these properties, just ask the bank's loan department what's available.

 The Bargain Hunter's [& Smart Consumer's] **Field Guide**

Finance Fever

Wow! You've bargained for, and bought, that dream property and you're ready to roll. Except now you need financing, which you can get through your bank, your credit union, or a mortgage lender. As a savvy bargain hunter and consumer, you can get a deal here as well, when you know how.

Make It Right

The first rule—as always—is do your homework. Bankers and other mortgage-lending types place a lot of weight on your credit rating. Which can be worse than you imagine, and often through no fault of your own. So you need time to make it right.

When you first get that new-house gleam in your eye, send for copies of your and your spouse's or significant other's credit reports. Two of the largest agencies are Experian, which you'll find online at www.experian.com/product/consumer/online.html or by phone at (888) 397-3742, and Equifax, which you'll find at www.equifax.com/consumers/consumers.html and (800) 685-1111.

As soon as you get your reports, give them a good going over. You may discover that the credit reporting agency has you down as defaulting on a loan you never took out or being 90 days late on a credit card you may or may not possess. These reports may also show you as the possessor of credit cards you haven't used in years or that you thought you'd cancelled years ago.

continued on page 174

Send a letter or fax to each credit bureau that has erroneous information requesting that they correct and repair the errors immediately. Also ask that they send you a copy of the corrected report so that you can verify they've made the fixes.

If you have not-so-nice information on your credit report that's valid, you can still take action. Write up an explanation and ask the bureau to attach it to your report. If you were late on several credit card payments a few years ago, for instance, you might explain that you were laid off from your job but that you've since had an impeccable record.

The credit bureau, by law, has to respond to your request within 30 days. Which is good. But if the bureau comes back and says that the bank you never heard of in East Zebulon, Ohio says you did default on a loan (and you didn't), you'll have to call the bank and get them to admit their error and notify the credit bureau.

You can see why you'll want to start on this right away. But all the work is worth it. Now when you go to the lender, you're ready, willing, and able to sign on the dotted line with a credit report that's as blameless as you can make it.

The seller lived several hundred miles away and had put it on the market when her mother, who owned it, passed away. She had listed it at $89,000, but—not surprisingly—hadn't found a buyer. We offered $50,000, along with a list of the property's flaws. The seller sputtered and balked, but after considering the actual condition of the place, agreed to our price. So we bought it.

It took a lot of work, but it was also a lot of fun. We transmogrified the ugly duckling on the block into a charming cottage, and three years later we sold it and the vacant lot for a total of $117,000, well over twice what we'd paid for them. We call that good bargain hunting!

[Attach an explanation of delinquent payments to your credit report to help correct your image.]

Major Minuses

What if you have major credit minuses that you can't gloss over? You've still got options. You can find a sympathetic lender—which can sometimes be done but takes a lot of work and a lot of shopping around. You can ask a friend or relative to co-sign the loan. (Just make sure you don't default and gum up their credit.) Or you can find a property with owner financing. This reduces your bargaining power to some degree, but doesn't put you entirely out of the game.

If you don't want to go for any of these options, find a terrific deal on a rental property, take the tenant route for a while longer, and make cleaning up your credit your goal. When you know what needs to be done, it's not so hard. And in the meantime, you can keep honing those bargaining skills.

Expedition Tip

Remember: The bank or mortgage broker views your ownership of lots of credit cards as an opportunity for you to rack up thousands of dollars in charges and take off for Tahiti without paying back a dime. So cancel all those cards you don't really want and keep just the few that are your bargain hunter's tools.

Head To Head With The Lender

Most people think that the banker or mortgage lender holds all the strings. And that's exactly what they'd like you to think. But it's not quite true. You can shop for a lender the same as you shop for any other product or service. And you can certainly bargain.

Where do you shop? Check out local banks and savings-and-loan associations, and your credit union (if you belong to one). You can also check out local mortgage bankers, which your real estate agent can recommend, as well as shop for mortgages online. The major point here is not to take the first lender that says he'll take you. As a savvy bargain seeker you've got options here, just like down at Wal-Mart.

What's to shop for? Look at the following:

* **Interest rates.** Bankers and other lender types live by the annual interest rate of a loan. Although they all stick to rates that are tied to various national or international indexes, you will find some flexibility. In other words, if the going rate in *The Wall Street Journal* is 8 percent, don't think you'll find a bank that will quote you 3 percent—that would give a lender apoplexy. But you'll find some that will quote 7 percent or 7.5 percent or 7.75 percent.

* **Points.** This is not the same kind of points as you find on vintage cars with condensers and carburetors, but instead refers to a percentage of the loan amount that the lender will ask you to pay when you close the loan. One point equals 1 percent, so if you take out a $100,000 loan with 2 points (or 2 percent), you get to pay the bank $2,000 for the privilege of borrowing the funds.

* **Fixed- or adjustable-rate mortgage (otherwise known as an ARM):** With a fixed-rate mortgage, your interest rate stays the same throughout the life of your loan. If you start off with an 8 percent interest rate, that's what you'll have 15 or 30 years down the time line. With an ARM, your rate starts out low, but changes or adjusts (hey, that's why they call it adjustable!) along with the going interest rates in the country. ARMs can change every six or 12 months or more frequently, depending on how your loan is written. So while you may start out paying less than the going rate, say 6 percent, you may find a year or two later that you're paying 10 percent or more. Or, if interest rates drop, you could find yourself paying only 4 percent—not likely, but possible.

  You might decide on an ARM instead of a fixed mortgage if you truly believe interest rates can only go down, or if you plan to be in that fixer for only a short time.

* **15- or 30-year loan.** Most lenders will cheerfully write you either a 15- or 30-year loan. The 15-year version obviously pays off in half the time, but the downside is that your payments are much higher.

* **Pre-payment penalty.** Lenders sometimes write in penalties of several points for paying off your loan early. (No, they don't want you to pay up. They want the interest.)

* **Balloon notes.** Some lenders, especially those making commercial loans, like to insist on balloon notes. While this sounds like something carefree and party-hearty, it's not. A balloon note or loan is one that's fairly short, usually from two to 10 years, as opposed to a standard 15 or 30 year loan. When the note comes due, in as little as two years, the bank can refinance your loan. Or they can call the note and ask that you pay the whole thing immediately. Gulp!

Expedition Tip

Like mattresses, loan rates and terms vary considerably. And like mattress manufacturers who change the outside covers and the names but not the inner components of their bedding, lenders often—and purposely—change the names of their products so it's hard to make comparisons. Don't let them fool you. Ask for the basics of what you want from each lender; then compare.

BUSINESS BEACON

Counter Intelligence

The terms you negotiate on a business loan will have a great impact on your bottom line, so it's crucial that you get terms you can live with. Don't take what the bank offers if it isn't what you want. Go ahead and counter-offer. The bank isn't going to crumple the loan documents and throw you out the door if you negotiate. In fact, you'll impress them. Bankers appreciate a savvy adversary. The fact that you're tough and wiley tells them you'll be the same way in business, which gives them more confidence in your abilities and your company.

Facts Of Life

As your business grows, so does your need for capital. Which means that as an entrepreneur, you often have to shop for loans. It's a fact of life. But what's also a fact of life (little understood by all but savvy bargain hunters) is that banks need you as much as you need them. They rely on a strong portfolio of loans to keep interest-bearing funds oiling their machinery. Bottom line: It's an equal partnership between you and the bank and you have a strong bargaining position.

Shop around. Do your homework. The bank where you already have an account may not be able to offer the best rates or terms—it depends on their portfolio and the types of loans they need. Like any smart business, they diversify and they may already have a full complement of the loan type you want, whether it be small business, real estate, home equity (borrowed to get your business going), or whatever.

Also, even if your bank wants to make you that loan, the regional office—which doesn't always understand your local market—may not approve it. So if you don't check with a variety of banks, you may find yourself high and dry without a loan at all.

Chapter Ten
Wrapping It Up

In and among all those shopping adventures, there also comes a time when, as they say in film-making, "It's a wrap." (Which the savvy shopper hears as, "Wrap it up; I'll take it.) This is the moment when you decide to sell your stuff, make a tidy profit, and—sometimes—give someone else a deal.

The Seven Rules Of Resale

There are secrets to selling those bargains, just as there to buying them. The quintessential advice, of course, is to "buy low/sell high." You've learned through the course of this book to accomplish the first half of this equation, but what about the second?

Follow along as we reveal how to make the most from your ready-to-recycle merchandise with these seven rules of resale:

1. **Know what you paid.** You can come up with a good sales price only when you know what the item cost you. There's no point in selling something for $10 if it cost you $15. Make up a simple filing system and keep receipts for everything you buy so you can refer back when necessary.

   For big-ticket items such as vehicles, it's important to keep a log of your expenses as well. Use a simple bookkeeping program, like Quicken, or keep a running tally, but add in everything that contributes to the cost. You'll want to start with the price of the car, then add in things like the fuel pump and filter you had replaced, those sheepskin seat covers, the custom dash cover, and even that clever driver's-side coffee cup holder. Keeping a list has an added benefit: It shows the buyer how much you've put into the car (bargaining chip for you) and demonstrates that you've added a lot to make it a good buy.

2.   **Know the value.** The amount you paid for an item is not necessarily the same as its value. You may have negotiated an absolute steal on something worth far more than the funds you handed over, or you may have paid a fair price at the time for a piece of merchandise that's not worth much at all today. So again, do your homeowrk and determine the current market value.

3.   **Know the demand.** Demand contributes a great deal to the value and price of a product. If you're selling vintage cuckoo clocks and everybody in your area is fixated on digital ones, you'll have a hard time getting a good price. On the other hand, if you're selling lava lamps (which you probably couldn't have given away five or 10 years ago), you can command a pretty penny.

4.   **Know how and where to market your merchandise.** There are different markets for different goods. An 1884 dining table priced to sell at $3,000 won't find a taker at a garage sale, while a 1984 mass-market dining set will be turned down by an appraiser from Sotheby's. People in different areas of the country have different tastes as well. A nifty Fifties kidney-shaped coffee table that's all the rage in Los Angeles may not find a buyer in lower Alabama.

5.   **Know how to present your products.** You'll get a better price when you merchandise your products. Dress them up and make them look like they're worth your buyers' money. Detail a car. Clean and press old clothes. Showcase small items like coins, jewelry, figurines, and even salt-and-pepper shakers on a velvet background or soft cloth. Make them look important.

6.   **Share what you know.** Everybody appreciates honesty. When you buy a car, computer, or TV set, you want to know about any glitches. As a seller, it's important to provide your purchaser with the same sort of information. It's not only the moral and legal thing to do, but it helps establish a trust that can often lead to a buy.

7. **Set a price that leaves room for bargaining.** It's not fair to highly over-inflate the price of your goods (besides which, you run the risk of not selling them at all). But do set your price high enough that you leave a little room for haggling. You want to bargain when you shop, so give your buyer the same privilege.

Treasure Selling Venues

There are almost as many venues for sellling your treasures as there are for buying them. You can't, of course, set up a booth at your local Wal-Mart or Home Depot, but you've got plenty of other options:

* Hold a garage sale
* Host a rummage sale to benefit a favorite nonprofit venture
* Take your goods to a consignment store
* Put stuff up for auction
* Place an ad in the local newspaper or shopper
* Sell at an Internet auction
* Post your products in the online classifieds

Glorious Gift-Giving

Another way to turn your bargains into someone else's treasure is by giving them away. It's been said that it's better to give than to receive, and sometimes that's true. What doesn't contribute to that warm, fuzzy feeling like giving someone a gift?

It needn't be for traditional occasions like Christmas, Chanukah, or birthdays. The very best gifts can be those given for no reason at all—delightful, serendipitous surprises that come from your heart instead of from the retailer's calendar of events.

We once found a set of refrigerator dishes—heavy pressed glass containers that were all the rage for leftovers before Tupperware came along. We wrapped them in sheets of 1945 newspaper we'd discovered that featured ads for the very same refrigerator dishes. We put them in a box, decked it out in cheery giftwrap and ribbon, and presented the box to Terry's mom, who collects vintage kitchenware. It's hard to say who enjoyed it more, her or us.

Bargain hunting for gifts is not only a great excuse for buying while out nosing around, it's also smart shopping. You can purchase spur-of-the-moment gifts as well as those earmarked for specific holidays and birthdays. When the winter holiday crunch comes around or you belatedly remember a friend's big day, you don't have to rush out to the store. You'll already have gifts on hand.

Designate a spot on the top shelf of your linen closet or in a bedroom drawer, and use it as a stash for future gifts. (The trick is to pick one place and stick to it—otherwise when holidays roll around, you forget where you stored it all.)

Really Wrapping It Up

Whether you're selling, buying, or gift-giving, bargain hunting is the way to go. Bargain hunting is the ultimate method for expanding your purchasing dollar—no matter what you're shopping for—and a terrific way to have fun while you're at it. Besides netting you a lot of good old materialistic *stuff*, it also springs open the door to adventure, nourishes your creativity, and encourages recycling—one of the best ways to help our planet stay green and healthy.

Once you've got bargain hunting in your blood, you're hooked for life. There are always new shopping worlds to be explored and new conquests to be made. You'll nose out fascinating nooks in every part of town and all over cyberspace, and turn every travel adventure into a bargain expedition as well.

So get out there and get hunting. Keep your eyes and ears open, your sense of humor honed, and your bargaining atennae tuned, and you'll find those terrific deals in even the most unexpected places.

Index

A

 The Bargain Hunter's [& Smart Consumer's] **Field Guide**

 The Bargain Hunter's [& Smart Consumer's] Field Guide